Leadership Lessons from 22 Yards

An interesting comparison of cricket
and corporate stories for entrepreneurs
and leaders to create high-performance teams
and winning culture.

Srikanth Ram

First published in 2021 by

Becomeshakespeare.com
One Point Six Technologies Pvt. Ltd.
119-123, 1st floor, Building No. J2, Wadala East,
Wadala Truck Terminal, Mumbai, Maharashtra 400037, India
T: +91 8080226699

ISBN 978-93-90463-99-2

Dedicated to my precious Poorni and Ria who have been
my rock, supportive of whatever I do.

Gratitude

First, I would like to thank you for picking this book. It is difficult for a new author like me to get patronage. I hope to deliver you immense value by the time you finish this book.

This book is not an effort of one person. I have a long list of people to thank because as it is my maiden book, I received enormous support from dear and near ones, far and wide.

My parents, Ramasundaram and Visalam, whom I miss every day but wake up to feel their blessings each morning. Their teachings have gotten me where I am today and more.

Pranam to all my gurus, coaches, and bosses at various organisations to have taught me the nuances of life, business, and most importantly, entrepreneurship.

My elder sisters, Raji and Anu and their families, my elder brother Ramesh and his family for their constant support and motivation throughout my life.

My uncle Ram (Chandru), who constantly encouraged me not only while writing this book, but through every aspect of my life.

My friend Akash Agarwal, a cricket aficionado and successful entrepreneur, who has encouraged me from the time I told him that I was writing a book on cricket. He constantly followed up with me at each and every stage of the book.

I owe deep gratitude to Mr. S.L Pokharna, President Commercial, and Mr K.A.Narayan, President HR, Raymond Limited, who have been pillars of support and the first people who encouraged me to write when they read my blogs.

My friend Ummed Singh, a cricket enthusiast and branding expert, founder of 'b brave', for suggesting the title of this book. After reading the initial manuscript, he made me think about a fictional story that prompted me to rewrite the entire book.

To all my friends who gave valuable feedback after reading the manuscript of this book, thank you for your help and suggestions.

Special thanks to my good old friend and the cricket captain of my team during my playing days, Ashok Anand for getting all the help from the cricket fraternity to validate my stories.

In a world of people asking 'what's in it for me?', Ajay Seth has a heart of pure gold. He coordinated with his good friend Dilip Vengsarkar to write the foreword for this book. It is hard to find people like him. Gratitude, Ajay.

I have immense gratitude for Dilip Vengsarkar for a wonderful foreword. When a debutant author writes, it's hard to get an endorsement. Not only did he write the foreword but also gave extraordinary inputs to make this book what it is today.

Every true cricket fan in India should be in awe and gratitude for the enormous contribution that they have made to Indian cricket. There could be a separate book on their contributions, yet they remain the true gentlemen servants of this gentleman's game.

I thank from my heart Lalchand Rajput, Prakash Iyer for their testimonials and directions.

More than a friend and part of my family, Jeeva and Kavitha for supporting and backing me all the time. My flying buddies Arif and Dr. Karnam for their encouragement. They are already pushing me to write my second book on my other passion, flying, which I am sure with their constant prodding will see the light of the day soon.

My team of editors, Vaibhav Pathare, and designers who diligently worked on the book to make it better.

I must thank the Become Shakespeare team: Malini Nair, Trupti, Sameer, and Pranali for constantly being in touch and ensuring all the small details are well taken care of.

Certainly not the least, I thank my critics. You help me to improve and keep me humble. I respect your inputs.

Preface

In the years that I have spent teaching, discussing, and motivating different teams in various organisations that I have worked, I realized that, subconsciously, the terms, incidents, and anecdotes that I use to support my hypothesis have often come from a sport very dear to us Indians – Cricket. And it worked both ways. It made some intricate concepts easier to understand for the participants and enjoyable for me to explain.

It helped that I had played a good amount of cricket. Although my cricketing achievements aren't much to talk about, I have always been a keen observer, which helped me to understand the intricacies of this great game. After a while, I began to understand the patterns in my thoughts and realized that cricket and business leadership are not that different after all. The only difference is that, unlike cricket captains, we don't see corporate leaders perform the act of leadership live at Wankhede Stadium.

Be it any field, it is surprisingly easy to identify good leaders; however, it's a monumental effort to define what constitutes good leadership. This thought has pinged me enough in recent times that I decided to put down my thoughts in the form of this book. I was kind of excited that I was going to get a chance to amalgamate two passions in my life – Business and Cricket.

As I researched more, combined with my experience of spending close to 3 decades working with entrepreneurs and leaders in large corporations, I realized that there is a process to building high performance teams and creating a winning culture. I was fascinated with the interesting stories, similarities between some of the business tycoons and cricketing stalwarts, their starting points, their ideals, their obstacles, their growth, their impact on society, and the leadership traits that we can learn from them. I have talked a lot about courage, innovation, resilience, steadfastness, perseverance, and other ingredients that make a good leader irrespective of the field of expertise.

We often see business leaders through the lens of the company balance sheet, failing to realize that these are just the results of an intangible element called *culture*. While the results do quantify a company's success, it would be futile to just focus on these numbers in isolation. It would be like judging a cricket team's captain only through the number of trophies won without understanding the *process* with which the team was built, the strategy that was applied, the players that were backed despite prior on-field performances, the decisions that were made when chips were down during a crucial stage of the tournament and so on. They say the devil is in the details and that is what I have tried to find during the research for this book.

The intangible, the *culture* or the *process,* is not built accidentally, especially not in case of long term success. It would be difficult for anyone to define organizational culture in a single sentence. Moreover, I don't think *culture* is something that needs a definition. It is something that needs to be experienced. A team experiences the culture by being a part of it, while the spectator experiences it through the team's public behaviour.

When a group of different individuals seems like a single unit on the field, the individual ceases to exist. Only the team exists. That's the result of the culture in the team. That is the invaluable, intangible result of the process they have painstakingly stuck to for many years. A leader is responsible for cultivating and nurturing that culture by leading from the front, by being everything that is expected from the team, by walking the talk, and then by being in the background when success eventually arrives.

It's a hard road, but as with other things in life, a true leader knows and does what needs to be done. When the moment arrives, a leader is mature enough to pass the baton along to the most deserving one. This is the most underrated but essential character of a leader.

A leader evolves along the way and lives his life through the successes and failures of the ones being led. It is simple, but it is not easy; otherwise, we wouldn't be facing a dearth of good leaders around us. But why wait for a good leader when you can become one? I do not believe that leaders are born. I believe they can be taught and trained.

Please read sequentially to get the best of this book. At the end of each chapter, I have added a few questions for the readers to answer. I would like you to introspect about your life and career. Contemplate on your life to understand those moments in which you felt you wanted to do something big, something that you dreamt about but could not take steps to achieve.

This is my humble attempt to bring to you some fascinating stories of leadership in business and cricket, delicately woven with a fictional story of two brothers building an organization. I hope the stories will touch the leader inside you to build your high performance teams and a winning culture.

Thank you!

Foreword

Leadership is to stand in the face of adversity and make rational decisions. I was playing against Pakistan in Delhi and we were chasing 390 runs in the second innings. It was a herculean task considering we managed only 126 odd runs in the first innings. We were getting closer to an impossible victory, but the fall of wickets at regular intervals made it difficult. I had a choice to make - go for a win and risk losing the match, or save the match by going for a draw. I made a calculated decision that going for a draw was the best scenario for India. We saved the Test and won the series 2-0 later on. In retrospect, it was a good decision.

Being in the moment, having an eye on the larger picture, knowing the purpose, being able to carry the weight of responsibility on your shoulders, having a rational approach to problems, and a strong belief in your core principles are as helpful on the cricket field as they are in any organization.

If you look at leadership this way, then it becomes obvious that skills developed "on-field" can be applied in another field. From that aspect, this book "Leadership Lessons From 22 Yards" adds immense value to understanding management and leadership in sports.

Indian cricket has a history of good administrators. If you take conscious efforts to spot young talent and nurture it, then you will see success in the long term. That's what we try to do at Vengsarkar Academy.

Over the years, BCCI has used different approaches to identify talent early; I was made the Chairman of the Talent Resource Development Wing (TRDW) when it was created in 2002 to develop talent.

Many successful players of the Indian team, including the World Cup-winning captain Mahendra Singh Dhoni, Suresh Raina, Irfan Pathan, Sreesanth, RP Singh, and Piyush Chawla were first recognized via the TRDW. I saw the spark in Virat Kohli and backed him early in his career, even when some wanted him out of the team. Today he is unarguably the best player in the world.

When you want to dominate the game of cricket at a global level for years to come, it becomes important to develop a pool of talent at the domestic level to choose from.

The development of coaching facilities at the district level, strong domestic league, and former international players guiding youngsters all helped in this purpose. This was the reason for the dominance of Australia and this is the reason India is excelling at the top level.

The job of the current generation is to sustain this dominance.

India never lacked talented players; it was the process that was tedious. The process of identifying talent is very well discussed in this book, reminding us that the fundamentals are the same whether it's business or sports.

This book has several anecdotes from cricket infused with management lessons. I find this book interesting as it chronicles the history of cricket in India from a fresh perspective. The leadership on the field and in-office tells us what went behind the scenes and what it takes to succeed at the highest level.

For young cricketers and entrepreneurs alike, it might serve as a useful guide to develop personality traits and managerial abilities useful in the long run.

I wish Srikanth success in all his endeavors and hope this work helps entrepreneurs to build a great team and culture.

DILIP VENGSARKAR

Mumbai

Date: 10 October 2020

Contents

Gratitude 7

Preface 10

Foreword 14

1. Goals– 1997 19

2. Resilience – 1999 28

3. IKIGAI - 2001 36

4. Building a Team - 2003 46

5. Building Trust - 2005 55

6. Defining Culture, Winning Mindset - 2008 71

7. Dreams Come True - 2011 82

8. Staying Grounded - 2014 91

9. Women Power – 2015 98

10. Finding Harmony – 2018 104

11. Baton Change - 2019 111

12. Winning at What Cost- 2020 118

About the Author 128

CHAPTER 1

Goals– 1997

It was drizzling outside as I looked through the window. The Nandi hospital in Mysore wasn't the best, but it was the one we could afford. My dad, Ramakrishna Acharya, was battling for life after suffering a heart attack. He could not digest the fact that his business partner had cheated him, leaving him with nothing.

It was a relationship of over a decade. Dad was handling production, while Salahuddin uncle, his partner, was taking care of sales and finance. Never had we thought his friend and partner would do something like this. Tears rolled down my eyes thinking of my dad and his hard work which gave all of us a comfortable life.

Appa had a calm demeanor and he was deeply spiritual. He never scolded my elder brother Sandeep or me for anything. He insisted that we have high principles and aim for lofty goals.

He had a sense of achievement after he got both my elder sisters Vidhya and Janu married in a grand manner. After this, Appa's undivided attention turned towards my brother and me. I was just ten then. He did not like me being a below-average student and was worried about me.

My thoughts came to an abrupt halt when the doctor touched me. "Sandeep?" I felt the warmth of the doctor's hand and panicked. What would it be this time?

"Yes doctor, I am Sandeep," said my brother, who was sitting a few yards away stepped forward. "Sandeep, I am Dr. Jha, the chief cardiologist. Your dad is not in great shape. We will decide on open heart surgery after 48 hours of observation of his condition."

Sandeep eagerly asked the doctor if we could see dad. "Yes, you can talk to him, but ensure that he doesn't feel stressed." Those words from the doctor churned my stomach. What? Will my Appa leave me? Nothing can happen to him. I shall go to Salahuddin uncle's house tomorrow and fight with him. Noticing my tears, Sandeep said, "Sanju, I want you to be brave; this is not the time to be emotional. It's the time to cheer Appa and give him confidence."

Sandeep was like Appa, always caring for me and giving advice.

We entered the ICU and saw Appa lying on a bed that was inclined. "Appa," Sandeep called out, touching his hand. Appa responded immediately with a twinkle in his eye as if he was waiting to talk to both of us.

Sandeep asked him to take it easy while he tried to sit. Appa did not heed his advice. Appa was frail, but he eagerly signaled both of us to sit beside him.

Appa looked at me and said, "I don't want either of you to talk to Salahuddin uncle about anything. If I curse him or fight with him, it means I don't respect the beautiful friendship I had with him. I treasure that friendship more than the money transaction or business I had with him. He has three daughters, unmarried, and one of them is mentally challenged. Probably he had some constraints, and he did not know how to tell me. I know how much I struggled to get Vidhya and Janu married. I did not have any clue about the hardship he went through for their marriage." He made us promise that we would not talk to Salahuddin uncle on this anymore.

He looked at Sandeep and asked about his plans for the future. Sandeep was in his final year of college doing his MBA in Bangalore and had just reached that evening hearing the news about Appa. Sandeep said, "Appa, we will talk in the morning, that is not important now." Appa did not pay any heed to him and said, "I want to talk to both of you."

I recalled the doctor asking us to not cause any stress to him. We were more stressed than Appa. He seemed to be quite cheerful. He again looked at Sandeep and said, "I know you want to start a business and become like N. R. Narayana Murthy (NRN) of Infosys," he turned to me, "and I know you want to be like Kapil Dev."

Sandeep was a big fan of NRN and wanted to be an entrepreneur. He was always attracted to the idea of helping people with knowledge and wealth creation. He was excellent at debates, and his oratory skills were remarkable. I have seen both Appa and Sandeep talk for long hours about philosophy, spirituality, and other intense topics, while anything on cricket always interested me.

"Kapil Dev and NRN came up because of the goals they had set for themselves. If you set a goal for yourself in life, you must achieve it - that is success. My goal was Vidhya's and Janu's marriage and a good education for both of you. Sanju, you have not taken life seriously yet. You *must* start setting clear goals and not just a dream to become someone. Dreams will not get you anywhere, only goals and hard work will."

I vividly remember it was 26th June 1983 when he asked me what I wanted to become. He knew the answer. I always dreamt of becoming a great cricketer. Just the previous day, India had made history by winning the 1983 World Cup.

I wanted to be a trendsetter like Kapil Dev. "You want to be an icon in cricket, and you want to be an entrepreneur," Appa said smilingly, looking at both of us.

He took a sip of water and started speaking in a low voice that only the three of us could hear. "When Kapil led India to victory at the 1983 World Cup, we witnessed an event which was undoubtedly the game-changer for Indian cricket. Kapil's Devils were universally recognized as world champions."

"Cricket is so popular today because India won the 1983 World Cup. Similarly, in IT, NRN seeded a small company that went on to inspire a multitude of entrepreneurs to think big. Not for nothing is NRN called the Father of the Indian IT dream.

"I read in an interview, NRN said that leadership is all about bringing transformational change. He led by example, bringing about a transformational change in the Indian IT industry as a whole and putting India on the global map.

"Likewise, Kapil was a harbinger of change, impacting cricket both in India and across the global cricketing world. While NRN maintained that leaders must display courage, character, commitment, and generosity. Kapil persuaded a bunch of individuals to believe in themselves and convinced them that they could beat West Indies, the defending world champions."

Early in the tournament, India (17/5) was in deep trouble against Zimbabwe. That brought out the best in the Indian captain. Playing with determination, Kapil scored an epic 175 runs to help India to make a remarkable turnaround. That remains the only century Kapil scored in his one-day international career.

Appa continued, "It was that commitment and self-belief that Kapil showed in that stupendous knock, which convinced his team members to unite as one and start believing in themselves. Speak to any cricketer from the current generation – Sachin Tendulkar, Anil Kumble, Rahul

Dravid, Sourav Ganguly, VVS Laxman – and ask them who or what inspired their childhood dreams. You can be certain that you will hear a mention of the 1983 world cup."

I remembered Sunil Gavaskar, a legend and another cricket idol of mine saying in an interview to NDTV, "Kapil, by sheer example, led others by the way he played and the flair he brought into the game; he showed other Indian fast bowlers the way ahead."

Appa resumed after another sip of water. "All the bowlers who came after him, whether it was Chetan Sharma or Javagal Srinath, it was only because Kapil showed the way."

"Did you know Sanju, Kapil is very generous too?" I was spellbound that he was speaking so much about cricket and understanding the game with such nuances. Appa continued, "After winning the World Cup, Kapil told the then team manager Abbas Ali Baig that all the gifts and rewards received were to be shared equally amongst the team members. Such sharing was a departure from tradition." I was wondering why Appa was talking about all this now.

Appa turned to Sandeep and said, "Similarly, NRN, who came from a middle-class family, became an unlikely corporate leader. While both men had modest upbringings, the way they rose to become game-changers was inspiring. Kapil is the world's only all-rounder to have scored 5000 test runs and taken over 400 test wickets. Correct Sanju?" Appa was giving me surprise after surprise. His stats were spot on.

"Kapil's courage and commitment to win are similar to NRN's. Both believed in themselves. After encountering failure in his first venture, NRN could have gone back to work for another employer. Instead, he identified a team of exceptional individuals who joined him in creating and shaping Infosys."

NRN is renowned for his ethical ways of doing business. He once explained the pain of being ethically straight forward in an era of licensing. "Sandeep, do you know the story of how NRN struggled to import computers? There was a strict licensing regime and to import a computer took him three years He went about 50 times to Delhi by train as he couldn't afford a flight."

"Just as NRN earned a reputation for integrity and fair practice, so did Kapil for his sportsmanship in the first match of the 1987 World Cup, in which Australia scored 268 against India. After the close of the innings, Kapil Dev agreed with the umpires to increase the score to 270 as a six during the innings was mistakenly signalled as a four. As it transpired, India in their reply scored 269, falling short of Australia's score by just one run. The Wisden Cricketers' Almanack reported that Kapil Dev's sportsmanship proved the deciding factor in a close-run match.

I remember it was a piece of hot news that Infosys employees, through stock options, have benefited to the extent of Rs 50,000 crores as the company distributed 27% of its equity among them. I could see that this conversation with Appa deeply impacted Sandeep.

Appa turned towards us and said, "Sandy and Sanju, I am proud of you both. You have high moral values," Appa's tone was spirited. "Whatever you do in your life should have high values and goals. Write your goals and differentiate them from dreams. Be trendsetters like Kapil Dev and NRN in your chosen fields."

Looking at both of us, Appa said, "You may wonder why I am saying all this. I have nothing more to look forward to than you both excelling in life. I want to retire and take Visalam on a pilgrimage if my health permits."

He reclined on his bed with Sandeep helping him. Just then, a nurse entered and asked us to leave as it was late. Sandeep told Appa that we would see him the next morning.

"I am an average person with many below-average attributes. My little story should be a confidence-booster for every average person in the world (so) that he or she can make a difference, at least in a small way, to this world. In the long run, I believe that honesty is the best policy. One can get away by being dishonest for the short term, but ultimately, honesty is what pays."

— Kapil Dev

"You can be anything you want to be, if only you believe with sufficient conviction and act in accordance with your faith; for whatever the mind can conceive and believe, the mind can achieve."

—Napoleon Hill

Action to readers.

1. What are your dreams/aspirations in life?

2. What is/are your goal(s) forward?

3. What beliefs do you think may be holding you back or hindering you from achieving your goals?

4. What is the one thing that you believe you could change about your past so you could have achieved more success now?

5. How do you define success in your life? Chart out a road map towards achieving your life goals.

CHAPTER 2

Resilience – 1999

There was an uneasy calm. Sandeep and I did not sleep the whole night. We were determined that once Appa was discharged, Sandeep would hunt for a job for three months as he finished the MBA. I told Sandeep that I was done with cricket and would start preparing for MBA like him.

Sandeep looked at me, puzzled. He was wondering how I could decide in such haste after having listened to Appa's talk. He knew how passionate I was about cricket. "Sandeep, I am now 24, I have not yet played for the state team and I have not been scoring well this season either. So, I don't think I will make it."

My mind was on what Appa taught me. He always insisted on living the 3D lifestyle.

- Discipline
- Determination
- Dedication

He would often say – If you are fully committed to your goals and vision, it will make you disciplined, determined, and dedicated.

I pensively looked at my watch, it was 4.45 am. Suddenly the head nurse was shouting for the on-duty doctor to come in, which baffled us. We tried to enter the ICU. The nurse stopped us. We were restless. The on-duty doctor came out of the ICU and told us that Appa had a massive heart attack, and was unconscious. We were shell-shocked. Appa was talking to us just a few hours ago. How could this be true? What is going on? Are they treating Appa properly? There were many doubts in my mind.

Around 5.30 am, the doctor came and gave me the biggest jolt of my life. Appa had passed away after the heart attack. It was the hardest situation I had ever faced. It was like a cricket ball hitting my head at 150 kmph. I was trembling. I felt as if my cricket was taken away. It was the feeling of someone very dear leaving me.

After the funeral ceremonies were over, Amma told Sandeep to finish college early and come back. I also started the same business that Appa was in. According to the promise made to Appa, Amma too said the same thing about Salahuddin uncle. We dropped the matter and did not speak to him.

With a capital of Rs 2 lakhs, I tried starting the plastic manufacturing business that Appa was in. I tried hard, but it was only failure that I could taste. Sandeep too joined me in the business, but still it was a failure. Sandeep tried to work for an MNC through my uncle's contact, but he was unsuccessful.

We again borrowed some money from our sisters, Vidhya and Janu, and started to manufacture and market household products for export. But this was for a short duration and this business too came to an end. Sandeep was good with photography and started taking pictures and thought he could keep us afloat, but in vain. By now, we had tried different businesses but were not successful.

We both were a wreck, trying different things only to end up in disaster. We had shifted from Mysore to Bangalore in the interim, thinking that it would yield some good traction to our business, but all we tasted was failure after failure.

It was in early 1997 on a cold evening. We were both sitting at the usual tea stall. For many days only tea was our food. We used to have six cups of tea during the entire day. We both were in despair. I had sheer reverence and gratitude to my parents for they were able to feed us so well and never made us go through the feeling of what it means to starve. "Sanju, dai Sanju," I could hear someone in the distance calling me; it was Janu's husband Karunamurthy. We called him Murthy Mama. He worked at a good position at an export firm. He took us to a nearby restaurant. It was the first good meal we had in many days. Sandeep and I had decided long back that we will not trouble Vidya or Janu by asking for further help after they had initially helped us in the export business. He could sense that we were in trouble.

Mama sensed from our conversation that we would not take any further money from him. We were talking about more of our failures and were in a negative mindset. He tried to encourage us by talking about cricket. He knew that would break the ice and started talking about Marvan Atapattu who had many failures too. Sandeep was curious. "Who is Attapattu?"

I began narrating the story of Atapattu. Making his debut in Test cricket for Sri Lanka, Marvan scored a duck in his first innings. And again a duck in his second innings.

"The selectors dropped him. He went back to the nets for more practice. More first-class cricket. More runs. Waiting for that elusive call. And after twenty-one months, he got a second chance.

"This time, he tried harder. His scores: 0 in the first innings, 1 in the second. Dropped again, he went back to the grind. And scored tonnes of runs in first-class cricket. Runs that seemed inadequate to erase the painful memories of the Test failures.

"Well, seventeen months later, opportunity knocked yet again. Marvan got to bat in both innings of the Test. His scores: 0 and 0. Back to the grind. Would the selectors ever give him another chance? They said he lacked big-match temperament.

"His technique wasn't good enough at the highest level. Undaunted, Marvan kept trying. Three years later, he got another chance. This time, he made runs and in an illustrious career thereafter, Marvan scored over 5000 runs for Sri Lanka. That included sixteen centuries and six double centuries.

"He captained his country. All this despite taking over six years to score his second run in Test cricket." I felt energized by narrating this story.

Mama added, "How many of us can handle failure like him? Six years of trying and failing. He must have been tempted to pursue another career. Change his sport, perhaps. Play county cricket. Or, oh well, just give up. But he didn't. And did you know that he is a qualified Chartered Accountant? He had the passion and more importantly, the self-belief that he would succeed. You both need to have that belief and determination."

Sandeep saw a poster of Amitabh Bachchan just outside the restaurant. His struggles always intrigued Sandeep. From being rejected for an audition at All India Radio to fight back from a near-fatal injury on the sets of the movie Coolie to failing in politics.

"This shows that it's not only the talent and skill but attitude that is the key ingredient to achieve greatness." It was like Appa talking in Murthy Mama's voice.

Mama has been watching cricket from much before me. He was a fan of Prasanna, B. S. Chandra, Venkataraghavan, and Bedi. He continued, "Cricket has seen many greats who have come from adversities. Mansoor Ali Khan Pataudi was one such legend. In his youth, Pataudi was at Oxford University, pursuing his undergraduate education. He was also then playing county cricket for Sussex, following in the footsteps of his illustrious father, Iftikhar Ali Khan Pataudi, who had represented both England and India in Test matches. Then suddenly, one day, the unthinkable happened.

"Pataudi Jr was accompanying his friend on a drive when he was involved in a head-on collision with an oncoming vehicle. Pataudi was hospitalized with multiple injuries. But when he was discharged a few days later, Pataudi discovered to his horror that he had lost sight in his left eye. The doctors had to implant an artificial eye in its place.

"In his autobiography titled Tiger's Tale, Pataudi recalled that when he played cricket for the first time after the accident, he could see two balls, about one foot apart from each other. To survive at the wicket, Tiger addressed the oncoming ball that was closer to the stumps and scored 36 runs before losing his wicket.

"Armed with just one eye and an indomitable spirit, Tiger Pataudi played for India, becoming at 21 India's youngest captain — a record that stands unbroken to this day. Apart from scoring over 2000 runs with six centuries, Pataudi became the first Indian captain to win a Test match, and a series, abroad, in New Zealand in 1967-68. India won the series 3-1. Most captains in Indian cricket then had a defensive mindset and aimed at not losing rather than winning. Pataudi earned a reputation for being a fearless skipper and a skipper who trains his team to attack and win rather than be defensive.

You must remember what he said in his Autobiography, and you must think of this whenever you face failures. *"I only lost my sight, not my vision."* Never lose your vision. Why are you both crestfallen? You have a lot to achieve in life; be brave and start again." Sandeep and I looked at each other. There was one thing we both immediately recollected. What Appa had said that night–you must have goals.

Mama's talk was like a balm to us. "I have some savings. I will lend you Rs 5 lakh. I have a friend who wants to sell his business of renting computers. It has a client base, and he cannot run it due to health issues. I think you can do well since it's a running business." That night, we came back home and started writing what we wanted to achieve. That was probably the turning point in our lives.

"Successful people demonstrate their resilience through their dedication to making progress every day, even if that progress is marginal."

— Jonathan Mills

Marvan Atapattu story courtesy Mr. Prakash Iyer - First Published in his book - The Habit of Winning.

Action to readers.

1. What are your failures and what are your learnings?

2. Did you give up too soon? Do you lack persistence?

3. If you could travel back in time what do you think are the reasons for you to give up? Do you think that reason is justified now?

4. If you are having the same reasons of the past as a challenge even today then you need to work on those with the 3 D's to succeed. If not then the reason is not justified as it would fade away with time as it has happened now.

CHAPTER 3

IKIGAI - 2001

Sandeep and I were thrilled to write down our goals. It was the first step we took to put our life in the right perspective.

Our goals read: By 2010, we create a huge IT organization, employing millions of people and creating wealth for many. We launch one of the biggest IPO ever in India and run a very profitable organization with high values and conduct business with honesty and integrity.

The money Mama had given us went a long way. We started small, and our first clients were Wipro and Infosys. The Y2K projects created a huge demand for hardware and software.

This was a good omen. Sandeep took care of the hardware rental business while I handled the software side of the business. The business began to flourish. In the space of two years, we had a staff of 24 compared to just 4 in the beginning.

'Bodhi' is the state of enlightenment attained by a Buddhist who has practiced the Eightfold Path and attained salvation.

That is what we named our company — Bodhi. So that we would never forget that all that we do is a part of an enlightenment process. I loved the name. We moved into more specified areas like application development and maintenance. We added data analysis as well as enterprise application services.

We won appreciation from many of our customers for prompt delivery and excellent customer service. Within a few years, we were clocking Rs 3 crores in revenue and 40% in profits. Then, in 2000, Sandeep got married to his long-time college friend. Life was good until Sandeep phoned me one lazy Sunday afternoon.

"Sanju, I want you to listen to me carefully. You know I don't take hasty decisions," he said. Whenever he began speaking like this, I always knew he was dead serious. "The days of struggling to make ends meet are over, I am proud of you and how you have handled the business. Honestly, I am still surprised you left cricket to focus on business."

It hit me like a thunderbolt, I was getting restless. "I need to pursue something I want for myself," he added. This didn't sound like the Sandeep I knew. "Motivational speaking and consulting have been my dream for a very long time. And I think now is the time for me to pursue it." I couldn't believe my ears.

"I am happy with how you've handled Bodhi, and I am sure you can take Bodhi higher. Permit me to walk my chosen path." That last sentence caught me off guard.

"Permission? To walk your chosen path?" I was shocked.

Yes, it was true. Sandeep knew that, and he was going to chase his dreams.

"Think of this for a few days and get back to me," Sandeep told me.

"Okay, I will." That request was relieving and threatening at the same time. His tone sounded like he had already made up his mind.

"I want you both to do what you love most," I recalled Amma had once told us this.

Over the next two days, I was thinking only about how to run the show without Sandeep. I knew Sandeep would be happy in his chosen field, and I did not want to be a hindrance. After all, he would still be a 50% shareholder. I could always go back to him when there was a need, and he would not be far away from me. I had a few conversations with Amma, which cleared my mind, and I gave my consent on one condition: that he would be there for me when I needed him.

"I will be there for you," he promised. He then placed his hand on my shoulder and said, "Ikigai." He took a pencil and a paper and began to draw four circles.

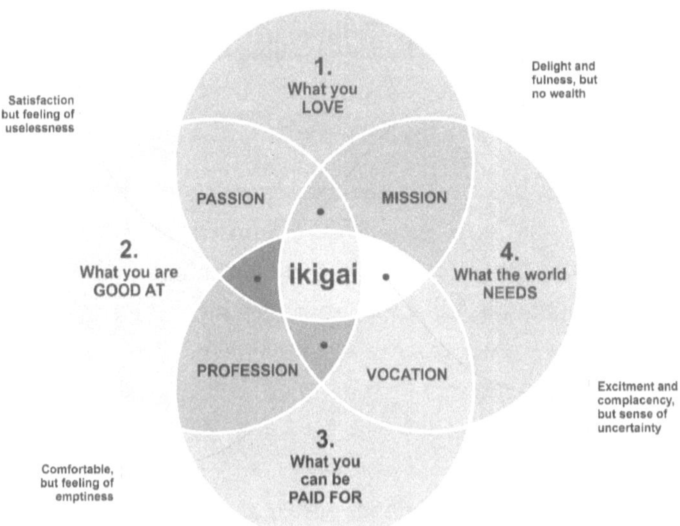

"Ikigai is a Japanese concept that means 'a reason for being.' The word refers to having a direction or a purpose in life. If your life has no path, you would be less motivated to do anything, even to lift a finger. There wouldn't be any reason to wake up from bed; there wouldn't be any reason to go to work. A life without direction is a life without meaning."

"These four circles are fundamental to identify one's Ikigai. Ikigai is the point where your passion, vocation, profession, and mission meet. Find your Ikigai. If one can find that balance, then living becomes enjoyable and reasonable."

I felt that at this point, I needed to find my Ikigai. Not that I didn't have a passion, or a profession and vocation, I needed to have a mission. Goals are time-based missions.

A year went by; the business was growing at a rapid pace. Sandeep was also establishing himself well with his captivating speaking, and already prominent corporates were signing for his thought leadership and consulting for Business Performance Improvements programme. I wanted to expand rapidly into other areas of business, such as Analytics, Digital Services, EAI BPM, Engineering R&D, Enterprise Application Services, Independent Testing, Infrastructure Management Services, etc. I knew it was difficult to expand into these areas unless I had substantial funding. I called Sandeep and asked him to advise me. He told me to consult Vineet Malhotra for financing, and Sandeep arranged for an appointment.

So, I went to Vineet's office at Mumbai Nariman Point. Vineet was in his late 50s. He listened intently and gave his advice. Like everyone who came across my idea, he was skeptical.

"I don't think you will be able to compete with the big sharks, Sanjay," he said.

"Firstly, you have no proper organizational structure and no team of professionals to run your business. You are still a one-man show," he added.

His words hit me hard. That was proof that they were right. He wasn't trying to discourage me, but only stating scary facts. I felt like a child in an ocean of sharks. Vineet called out for his office staff, "Sachin, arey Sachin chai leke aa."

My wandering mind went to the cricket field immediately. Did Sachin become an iconic cricket star overnight? No. He reached that level through a series of hardworking baby steps.

We were interrupted by a phone call for Vineet, so I had time to think through for a while. My mind was fixed on Sachin and his early days. I recalled an instance of Sachin.

India had done so well in the three previous Test matches of the series in 1989 and could play for a draw. In the 4th Test, at Sialkot, Pakistan, on the last day, a 16-year-old lad, Sachin Ramesh Tendulkar, came to bat when India was reeling at 38 for 4. He made his debut in that series.

The second delivery Sachin faced was of Waqar Younis and it was a short-pitched ball. Sachin tried to hook, got an inside edge, and hit his nose. It looked like a nasty injury. Within seconds Sachin's white T-shirt was splattered with blood.

The blood from a deep cut on the nose was still oozing, while Pakistani players were intimidating Sachin saying that was the end of his career. Some players recommended that he retire hurt. That would be curtains for the Indian dream of not losing a Test series in Pakistan.

The other batsman Navjot Sidhu and Team Physio ran to Sachin for help and were telling him to retire and get some first aid.

Just when everyone in the cricket field thought that Sachin would retreat to the pavilion, the master scrambled up and said in a squeaky voice —

"Mein khelega! Mein khelega!!!"

("I will play! I will play!!!")

The little master insisted that he would continue to play and refused to walk off retired hurt. He scored 57 runs from 134 balls and helped India draw the match and thus the series.

Vineet's office had a photo frame, **"When we least expect it, life sets us a challenge to test our courage and willingness to change; at such a moment, there is no point in pretending that nothing has happened or in saying that we are not yet ready. The challenge will not wait. Life does not look back." - Paulo Coelho**

"Sanju, it is tough to compete with these big companies as they are already established," Vineet told me after ending his call.

I bit my teeth. "Mein khelega. . . mein khelega…"

I murmured and got up to leave the meeting abruptly. Vineet was puzzled.

Vineet never knew he had added another goal to my list. I needed to build a world-class organization. He made me find my Ikigai.

"Young people often say "My life has no ikigai". This is obvious. People who isolate themselves can't have ikigai – meaning or purpose. Meaning and purpose are only found in interpersonal relationships."

–Tatsuzō Ishikawa

Action to Readers.

1. What is your Ikigai?

2. Another model of Ikigai – ask yourself:

   ➢ Who you are?

   ➢ What you do?

   ➢ Who you do it for?

   ➢ What those people want and need?

   ➢ And how they change as a result?

3. What is your goal in life?

Finding your "why" is important not only for success in your professional and personal life, but also for your well-being and longevity.

12 Steps to find your "why" in life

1. Identify the things you can do to make other people's lives better.

2. Think back to the activities you did that made you forget about the passage of time.

3. Recall what you liked to do when you were a kid.

4. Think about the things that you are willing to do even if you look like a fool.

5. Observe what people ask of you when they come to you for help.

6. Imagine what you would be doing if you learned that you only had a year left to live.

7. Enumerate the things for which you would be willing to go the extra mile.

8. If you were given the chance to teach others (e.g., young people), what would you teach them?

9. What task at work would you do for free if you didn't need the paycheck?

10. What's usually the reason why people thank you?

11. If you were given the chance to do something that you love and not worry about the paycheck, what would it be?

12. What was the happiest memory of your childhood?

CHAPTER 4

Building a Team - 2003

I must thank Vineet for giving us the clarity that we didn't have a professional team, and that I was running every department though we had an informal structure and department heads.

Sandeep concurred with me that we had to build a good team before going for funding discussions. We needed to show that it's an organization run by professionals. Sandeep told me that he was coming down to Bangalore on a client visit. He had moved to Mumbai as most of his clients were based there.

I got married in the spring of 2002 to Pooja, a girl known to my family. She also started assisting me in my business. We were determined to take this organization to great heights.

I met Sandeep at the Taj West End in Bangalore where he was staying.

My mind was on how to build my formidable team.

Cricket highlights of the ongoing World Cup were on TV at the coffee shop. Sandeep walked in, "What do you think? Will India take the Cup?" He asked me.

I opined that Saurav and his team had done well and they had a good chance. He said, "The Australians have a daunting side and they will give India a run for their money."

Steve Waugh was the captain of the Australian team and had created a great lineup and had succeeded in their goal of being the best cricket team in the world which was once dominated by the mighty West Indies.

He continued, "There are leaders like Anand Mahindra who have built a great team and we should learn from their experiences in putting a world-class team at Bodhi." While Sandeep was talking about the corporate leaders, my mind was transfixed on Steve Waugh. My cricketing brain was working at its best.

"The hallmark of these two self-made leaders had been their ability to create winning teams," Sandeep said and went to get his breakfast from the buffet spread. My mind was fixed on Steve Waugh's achievement in building a great team.

Australians have long dominated cricket, and one reason for this is the quality of captains they have been blessed with in the past. Thus far, Steve Waugh is arguably in the topmost slot. With a scientific and strategic outlook towards the game, Steve led his side to victory in the World Cup in 1999. Under Waugh's captaincy, Australia registered an unprecedented record of 16 consecutive test victories in 1999-2000. Steve

Waugh captained Australia in 57 Tests and registered 41 Test wins, the highest winning percentage in history.

Under his leadership, Australia entrenched its position as the best cricket nation in both the long and the short forms of the game. To achieve this, Steve worked hard to weave a team of high achievers and most importantly encouraged them to aspire for something great.

Waugh would urge his players to imagine they were part of a second-ranked team to ensure that they saw room for continual improvement and not get complacent.

Without a doubt, Waugh changed the way modern cricket is played, particularly Test cricket. It was on his watch that cricket saw the efficacy of a data analyst, a diet plan for each player, a detailed game plan, and a video analyst who would analyze the weaknesses and strengths of each opposition player which would help them to make a game plan to deal with each rival player.

My thoughts came back to the coffee shop as Sandeep started saying, "The journey of Mahindra & Mahindra (M&M) has been similar to that of independent India. The company began operations as a steel trading company called Mahindra & Muhammed in Ludhiana, on October 2, 1945. After independence, the name was changed to Mahindra & Mahindra and the firm moved into manufacturing and selling larger MUVs, starting with the assembly in India, under the license of Willys Jeep.

My mind was on cricket and Waugh. Steve was known for his team-building skills. I remembered what Justin Langer, another Australian cricket legend who played under Steve, wrote fondly of Waugh, "Steve was a leader for the people. Steve often challenged the group to be your own captain, to think for yourself, and to think on your feet. He would convince you that every step you take on the field should be in a forward direction. So, you make up your own minds."

I quickly cut my thoughts to listen to what Sandeep was saying. "Anand Mahindra has nurtured many well organized and productive teams. When Anand took over as the Deputy Managing Director of the Mahindra & Mahindra Group in 1991, the organization's activity was limited to the manufacture of automobiles and tractors. On Anand's watch, M&M expanded its business reach into such varied sectors as aerospace, agri industry, automotive, boats, hospitality, information technology, insurance broking, real estate and infrastructure, finance, steel, trucks and buses, two-wheelers, vehicle and equipment finance, etc."

Sandeep quoted Anand's own words reading from an interview I presumed, "It's not like I prescribed a plan to get this done. Everyone who works with us is encouraged to explore and contribute. Our job in the corporate sector is to create exposure to new concepts, spark conversations among the various elements in the group, and continuously enrich the ecosystem with ideas. The questions are: Who is catching these ideas? Who is taking them further? This becomes a way to describe great leadership: no prescriptions. Instead, create a rich environment for growth–everyone's growth. The person who is skilled enough to grab those nutrients is probably your future leader."

"Today," Sandeep elaborated, "each of these businesses is managed by a very competent CEO. One can imagine the tremendous effort Anand Mahindra must have put into fostering and nurturing such a highly motivated and skilled team in the conglomerate."

How did Anand Mahindra turn things around? I was wondering as Sandeep narrated Anand Mahindra's story.

Sandeep read further from the paper he had in his hand, "I have believed that if indeed a leader is empathetic and empowering, and delegates, then you have to make sure that people whom you have chosen to lead also show and follow that principle. Innovation only happens in an organization where its people feel empowered, understood, and trusted with the work delegated to them. People do not innovate in a climate of fear, hierarchy, or bureaucracy. In a hyper-competitive world, the benefit of innovation is an obvious one. You have to position empathy as a critical element in building a more innovative organization. But you can't make people sit down and read them the riot act and say, "You will have empathy now."

You hope that the leaders you appoint will combine the experience and the functional skills they need to manage with empathy. If they lack understanding, then one has to converse with them on why that element is essential. That today, is any leader's major role.

"Sandeep we are on the cusp of placing a good team at Bodhi, we can look for all the talents we need while recruiting newly but we have old senior employees with us, before we hire new senior leaders, can we look at evaluating them and promoting them?"

"Yes" agreed Sandeep.

How do we promote the existing seniors into the leadership positions?" I asked.

"Select a leader who gives credit to others when he is appreciated, recognized, and awarded. This will show if he is a team player. A good leader first is a good captain.

"Observe his clarity of thoughts while executing a plan. Is he wavering with his viewpoint? How does he conduct his meetings? Is he organized well in the meetings with a clear agenda, lets ideas flow, and never lets the meeting go off track?

"Does he command respect from his seniors?

"Evaluate the speed with which he gets things done while executing his plans or project.

"All these will show his ability, working with people, planning skills and resource management"

Sandeep's eyes lit up when he said, "Sanju you should note this, Anand advises youngsters to adopt a simple mantra:

"H B S." In acronym, H stands for Humility, B stands for Brevity - being brief and biased towards simplicity; simplify things that you do. S stands for Self-Awareness; you have to be aware of why you are doing what you are doing."

Sandeep recalled that when he casually met Bharat Doshi, CFO of Mahindra Group on a flight what he had to share about Anand Mahindra. "When I went to (the) Kandivali plant, he would come with me on the train when he could very well have taken his car. That was the kind of humble person Anand was. So, my reaction was (that) he was a friend, not a boss; he is also a mentor in a way. Some of the energy he created makes a huge impact on all of us."

I know Steve Waugh also has a very straight forward advice for Gen Y: Work very hard. He reminds everyone of four things successful people never say: should have, could have, would have, might have. Another striking similarity between Anand and Steve is that both are highly involved in philanthropy and very committed to the education of girl children.

Sandeep summarized beautifully that it's not just gathering a bunch of people and calling it a team. You need to focus on building a team that is dependable and skilled enough to deliver larger enterprise objectives. Building trust among them in achieving that goal is the essence of team building.

"In determining the right people, the good-to-great companies placed greater weight on character attributes than on specific educational background, practical skills, specialized knowledge, or work experience."

-Jim Collins,
Business consultant and author of Good to Great

Action to readers.

1. Do you do everything in your business by yourself?

2. Are you involved in every decision of your business?

3. Are you spending more time on tactical rather than strategic aspects?

4. Do you feel paying salary to your staff is a big achievement every month?

5. Are you firefighting most of the time?

6. Do you find it difficult to manage your team and set clear goals for them?

7. Do you find it difficult to measure your team's performance?

8. Do you find it difficult to make a data-driven decision?

9. Do you have to micro-manage each team member?

10. Do you have difficulty in identifying effective training and mentoring for your team?

11. Don't you have freedom from work?

If you have answered yes to most of the above, then you need to identify a business coach/life coach who can help you.

CHAPTER 5

Building Trust - 2005

The business was rapidly growing, and I was firmly in the saddle. Pooja delivered a girl, and we were thrilled with the new arrival in the family. We named her Tara.

Sandeep was blessed with two boys and he too was having an amazing time in consulting for not only the top companies in India but also for MNCs such as Microsoft, Oracle, and SAP. He was the most sought-after motivational speaker in Asia. My mother was very proud of both of us.

Sandeep and I had to put a team together. I wanted Sandeep to be part of the key selections made for the team. We took a long time to know each person and carefully inducted them into the organization. It was akin to selecting a cricket team. The selection had more weightage on attitude and adaptability than skill and knowledge.

The usual interview questions were, "How do you face success and failure?" But there were points that Sandeep insisted on knowing from all the candidates as to how they achieved what they had. He was interested in the story. He insisted on hearing about their vulnerable times in personal life.

'You need to learn to see into a person.' He told me. He explained the art of seeing below the water while referring to the Iceberg model. He continued, "hire and promote people to management positions if they're capable of forming positive interpersonal relationships."

An iceberg is something that is small at the top and larger at the bottom and as you go deeper it's stronger. It's important to see in a person what is below that water line and that is not easy. The below illustration will make you understand better.

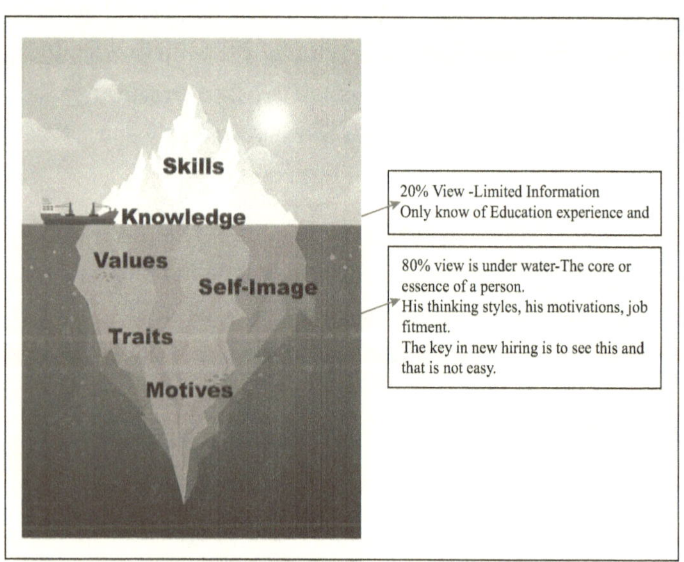

In an interview, Sandeep would quickly go into questions like, "Who is your role model?" and did not waste much time on questions like "tell me about yourself" etc.

Another powerful question was whom do you like to spend your time with?

Remember the company makes the man.

He was harsh when he was negotiating salaries and compensations. I asked him why he is haggling so much on compensations and eventually when we hired, he would recommend giving more. He said something impactful. *In life and business, you don't get what you deserve, you get what you negotiate.*

If the head of the department cannot negotiate for himself well, what will he negotiate for his organization?

Ability to adapt to change was another question he was incisive on. He would interview a very senior finance person and say in about 18 months time if we ask you to head marketing what would you say?

The answer would give insight on how this person is adaptable to change which is a major barrier in teams once hired. The more people willing to change in an organisation, more nimble the organisation will be.

The interview was fun and mentally challenging as it did not have the rather mundane recruitment questions.

Finally, we put a team that was a blend of people who had worked with us for long and some freshers. Each of them was given a significant shareholding in the company. We also rolled out ESOPs (Employee stock ownership plans) across the group having over 900 employees in eight locations.

Our new management team sounded like a cricket team to me.

1. Sachin Chandilya, who was with us from the beginning taking care of business and finance, was made Group Head of Finance.

2. Surender Megwah was newly inducted to head marketing.

3. Siddhartha Sambir who was Head of Sales was elevated as Group Head of Sales.

4. Suresh Naina was hired laterally and handed over charge of HR.

5. Balraj Singh who had served us for long was made Group Head of R&D.

6. Bharat Malli was elevated as Group Head, Operations.

I picked Sandeep's brain by asking him about who he thinks in the Indian corporate world has built a team on trust and has given people the freedom to execute strategies. He thought for a while and said, "There are many leaders who have very trustworthy leaders in their organization, but to me, Kumar Mangalam Birla (KMB) stands out."

Sandeep energetically explained, "A leadership role was thrust upon KMB after his father's sudden demise in 1995. He was just 28, and the challenge became even more daunting as he was required to fill the shoes of a man who was a legend in his own right and had become a God-like figure to his employees. The Aditya Birla (AB) group was already well known and there were many seniors not only in age but in experience too. The pressure of expectation was palpable.

"The press stopped short of calling him a donkey who was pushed suddenly into the deep end of the pool. KMB realized that he had very little time to learn how to swim. He was a chartered accountant with an MBA to boot. Additionally, he had spent five years working alongside his father."

I interrupted as the story sounded similar to that of our own Dada, Saurav Ganguly.

Sandeep smiled noticing that my mind had gone to cricket again.

"Yes, Sandy, like KMB, Saurav Ganguly was suddenly thrust into a leadership position at a very unexpected time. Sachin Tendulkar, who had succeeded Azharuddin at the helm after the match-fixing scandal, decided that it would serve the team's interest better if he focused on his batting without the distraction of captaincy. Saurav, who had served as Sachin's vice-captain was offered the top job. Dada grabbed the opportunity as he was already a settled player in the team, but the captaincy came at an unexpected time when cricket was riddled with the match-fixing scandal.

Sandeep acknowledged the similarity and continued, "Initially, KMB met with some opposition but managed to win over people with the transparency of his actions. KMB understood the importance of teamwork in creating a successful organization. He famously said —We need star teams, not just stars."

"Adapting to the need of changing times, within a decade, KMB managed to reduce the average age of employees in the group to 36 years, down from 56 years in 1995.

"KMB realized early that the people who worked for the AB Group were its strength.

"He knew that it was important to be genuine, in intent and effort, if he wanted to achieve genuine results. He believed that an energized workforce and the value of transparency would help him to cover the distance between good to great."

My mind wandered into cricket and Dada's captaincy.

I recounted, "During the nineties, India under Azhar had done reasonably well. When Azhar's career came to its close, the Hyderabad batsman had registered the most Test wins (14) by an Indian captain. However, most of those wins had come in home matches. A *sense of purpose* drove Dada as he sought to make India successful while playing away from home."

"Dada was known for his plain-speaking demonstrating his transparency like KMB. Ganguly's impeccable integrity and transparency won the day. His feisty aggression became infectious; where once Indian players had taken sledging on the field of play with a dose of forbearance and tolerance, they learned from Dada that they could pay back outwardly aggressive rival teams, such as Australia, in their own coin."

"No longer distracted by on-field tactics aimed at disturbing their focus, Saurav's men began to fight fire with fire. And rival teams began to sit up and take notice."

"He demonstrated that he could be a leader of a team which had greats like Sachin and Dravid in the side. Under Ganguly's leadership, India started winning matches and tournaments, which was lacking previously. Whether in his communication with fans or media or critics, Ganguly commanded respect with his candid and transparent style."

"He instilled self-belief in team members that they too could do well overseas. The likes of Virender Sehwag, Yuvraj Singh, Harbhajan Singh, Zaheer Khan, Dhoni—all blossomed under Ganguly's captaincy."

Sandeep enthusiastically said, "KMB understood that he could tap his team's creative potential by being adaptive and innovative. He set his sights on transforming what was a traditional Marwari business into a global conglomerate with innovations by starting an outreach program called Bizlabs."

I added, "Yes, innovation and building player skills is what Sourav did." Sandeep was too engrossed in the conversation and inquisitively asked, "What did Dada innovate in cricket?"

I answered, "For instance, Sourav asked Rahul Dravid to don the gloves as finding a permanent wicket-keeper had become a headache. Reluctant Dravid, who was one of India's most reliable top-order batsmen then, had no choice but to obey his captain's command. The move turned out to be a successful one.

"Virender Sehwag had batted in the middle order all his life. Even when he made his Test debut for India at Bloemfontein in South Africa, he had smashed a century batting at No. 6. But Ganguly saw something that many couldn't. He asked Sehwag to open the batting for India as he believed the Delhi right-hander's batting would bring more results at the top of the order. The rest as they say is history. He selected Dhoni later on promoting him to No. 3 Vs Pakistan.

"By the time Ganguly hung up his boots, he had emerged as the most successful Indian captain in both Tests and ODIs, whether at home or abroad. Like KMB, he had been initiated into the leadership game through baptism by fire. Like KMB, he emerged unscathed and victorious. As KMB was fond of reiterating - tough times don't last; tough people do."

It was another interesting conversation I had with my mentor-brother. To check if I had understood well the aspects of trust, Sandeep asked me to summarize the learning of building trust in the team.

- Hire properly.

- Demonstrate your trust in the team by empowering them.

- Be transparent and align the team to a larger purpose that they would aspire to be.

- Instill self-confidence in team members.

- Be genuine in intent and effort, be unbiased.

- Take thoughtful risks and back the team fully.

- Respect every team member.

    Sandeep acknowledged that all the above are ingredients for building trust "but there is one important point" he said.

- **To Build Trust, You Need to Keep Your Expectations High.**

    I was puzzled at this. Wasn't this counter productive?

    "By keeping high expectations, won't the team be demoralized?"

He said "no" and continued, "There is a difference between keeping high expectations and unrealistic expectations."

"It is only the weak leaders who expect little from their teams, and inevitably they *get* little. This phenomenon is often known as "the Golem effect.""

"Golem effect?" I questioned.

"The Golem effect has been demonstrated countless times in classrooms. If teachers think students are dull or incompetent, the students are generally not going to expend effort trying to prove their teachers wrong."

"It's essentially the opposite of the Pygmalion effect which has also been demonstrated in classrooms: when teachers expect good performance from students, the students' performance tends to rise to the challenge."

"You'll see both these phenomena in the workplace as well. Hence, it's good to have high expectations from employees, because they will tend to go on to fulfill those expectations. There is, however, a limit. Once high expectations cross the line into unrealistic expectations, consequences can be disastrous."

"When expectations repeatedly rise to where employees can never reach them, they will eventually think, 'Why bother?' After all, if putting in huge effort gets the same result (disappointment from their leader) as putting in minimal effort, why would anyone continue to push themselves? Once high standards become unrealistic standards, they become weapons, and results in:

- Low morale

- A "why bother" attitude

- Loss of respect for leadership

- High staff turnover"

"You don't want to be seen as a weak leader with unrealistically high expectations. You must have the right balance and that is not easy."

"When you set high expectations, the team will see that you trust them on their skill to attain that goal. However, in equal measure, you must demonstrate that trust too."

Restlessly I asked him, "How do I demonstrate that?"

He quietly said, "Put your skin in the game. Move from a contact leader to a connected leader."

"Connected leader?" I asked.

"Yes," he said. "Let me tell you the story of a monk.

"An Indian monk was interviewed by a journalist from New York.

Journalist — "Sir, in your last lecture, you told us about contact and connection. It's really confusing. Can you explain?"

The monk smiled and deviating from the question asked the journalist: "Are you from New York?"

Journalist — "Yeah."

Monk — "Who are there at home?" The journalist felt that the monk was trying to avoid answering his question since this was a very personal and unwarranted question.

Journalist - "My mother has expired. Father is there. Three brothers and one sister. All married..." The monk, with a smile on his face, asked again: -

"Do you talk to your father?" The journalist looked visibly annoyed.

The monk - "When did you talk to him last?"

The journalist, suppressing his annoyance said: "Maybe a month ago."

The monk: "Do you brothers and sisters meet often? When did you meet last as a family gathering?"

At this point, sweat appeared on the forehead of the journalist. Now who is conducting the interview, the monk or the journalist?

It seemed that the monk was interviewing the journalist. With a sigh, the journalist said: "We met last at Christmas two years ago."

Monk - "How many days did you all stay together?"

The journalist wiping the sweat on his brow said: "Three days."

Monk - "How much time did you spend with your father, sitting right beside him?"

The journalist looking perplexed and embarrassed and started scribbling something on a paper.

Monk - "Did you have breakfast, lunch, or dinner together? Did you ask how he was? Did you ask how his days are passing after your mother's death?"

Drops of tears started to flow from the eyes of the journalist.

The monk held the hand of the journalist and said, "Don't be embarrassed, upset or sad. I am sorry if I have hurt you unknowingly...

But this is the answer to your question about "contact and connection". You have 'contact' with your father but you don't have a 'connection' with him. You are not connected to him. The connection is between heart and heart - sitting together, sharing meals and caring for each other; touching, shaking hands, having eye contact, spending some time together. You brothers and sisters have 'contact' but you have no 'connection' with each other...."

The journalist wiped his eyes and said: "thank you for teaching me a fine and unforgettable lesson."

This is the reality today. Whether at home or in society or at work everybody has contacts but there is no connection. No communication, everybody is in his or her world.

Let us not maintain just "contacts" but let us remain "connected"; caring, sharing, and spending time with all our dear ones.

The monk was none other than **Swami Vivekananda.**

"Work isn't just about having a job to earn some money anymore. Most people need and want more than to just turn up, get their work done, and go home again. They want work they find meaningful, they want to feel like they have a shared purpose and want the work that they do to be valued. So, how we can increase how connected our employees feel is important.

"Simple things like finding out who they are in real life. What are their interests, what did they do over the weekend, and what do they find truly motivates them? Find out the challenges they are facing - at work and home, help them to hone their skills or to develop their interests in a way that sparks joy for them. In short, treat them like human beings– human beings you'd like to stick around for a long time.

"Remember to show that you are human too. Show your vulnerability, ask for help when you need it, and build bonds with people up, down, and every which way around you. Honesty will breed honesty. People with managers who are willing to say out loud that they need help will build deeper, more connected relationships. These people will be better placed to rise to a challenge, taking more ownership, more responsibility, and more interest when you need them to.

"Once you do this, all the above that we spoke about comes to you easily. The two leaders that we spoke about did that and that is why they were able to achieve what they have achieved. There was a shared purpose, not something different to each of the stakeholders i.e., customers, employees, and shareholders.

"Each of them puts the skin in the game and it starts with the leader."

I decided that I would demonstrate that my skin was in the game by aiming for something phenomenal for myself and my team.

Valuation and public listing of Bodhi will be 'my skin' in the game.

"Teamwork begins by building trust. And the only way to do that is to overcome our need for invulnerability."

– Patrick Lencioni

Action to Readers

1. Did you hire well?

    One of the common problems of entrepreneurs is the old employees who are disengaged.

2. Do you have this problem?

    The connection is the only key to turnaround the engagement with old employees. Understand the learning needs of these employees and invest in them to improve.

3. What is your and your team's shared purpose?

4. Is it creating value for customers, employees, and promoters?

5. Are you a connected leader? Do you know your People well enough?

6. Do you know the personal dreams/goals and aspirations of each of your team members?

CHAPTER 6

Defining Culture, Winning Mindset - 2008

On September 24, 2007, India unexpectedly won the T20 World Cup in South Africa. I always wondered how Dhoni handed the ball in the final over to a largely unknown and unheralded player from Rohtak—Joginder Sharma—with Pakistan needing 13 to win. I had a chance meeting on a flight to meet Joginder Sharma and asked about the moment he got the ball from Dhoni.

"While Dhoni played domestic cricket for Jharkhand, I was playing for Haryana. Our paths had crossed many times in domestic cricket, and he knew my qualities as a player going into the World T20, where many of the big names were not playing for India. The way he handled a bunch of new and young cricketers showed the self-confidence he had. He made a plan, and he followed it."

"Most people remember that I bowled the final of the title clash in 2007, but many don't remember that I had also bowled the final over in the semi-final against Australia. They needed 22 runs but could score only six and I got two wickets, Brett Lee and Michael Hussey. RP Singh had bowled the second last over in the semi-final and he bowled the second-last over in the final against Pakistan too. It was always following the plan that gave the results for Dhoni."

"So, when the time came in the final, Dhoni did not hesitate before giving me the ball. Pakistan needed 13 runs from the last over. I bowled a wide first ball, the second ball was a Dot ball and the third ball was a six. MS came to me and told me, don't think about the runs that they need, think about your bowling. If you get hit, don't over-think, just concentrate on the next ball. Whatever is the result, be confident you have my support.

He knew every player's strength and backed them to the hilt. He was a connected leader."

I could relate well now to what Sandeep told me a few months back. This was a reinforcement.

A few months later, I was enjoying the match of India Vs England ODI, when I heard Mumbai was attacked. I could not believe the news. Initially, I felt it was a rumour. But when I saw it on the TV, I could not believe my eyes.

Sandeep and I took a vacation with our families in Singapore for New Year's Eve. There had been a lot of negativity after the 26/11 attack and the financial meltdown, etc.

We also needed a break to spend some quality time with our families. Amma too was getting old.

On a late chilly night at the dinner table, Sandeep reminded me of our little goal that we wrote in 2000. How can I ever forget it? Every step and decision we took was with this destination in mind.

By 2010, we built a massive IT company employing hundreds and thousands of people and created wealth for many. We launched one of the biggest IPOs ever in India and ran a profitable organization with honesty and integrity.

Sandeep calmly said we are ready for the next orbit.

"Next orbit??" I asked.

"Yes, next orbit," he replied. "We have built a large IT company, but it is time we prepare for the IPO and create wealth for people around us and for ourselves and most important to crystalize the values we uphold as an organization.

"None can destroy iron, but its own rust can. Likewise, none can destroy a person but his own mindset can," said Sandeep who was enjoying these words of immense wisdom, quoting Ratan Tata. Sandeep had met Ratan Tata recently and was moved by his humility. For me, it was as if I had met Sachin Tendulkar.

The mindset that Ratan Tata and Sachin Tendulkar possess is why such unassuming people are regarded as great and humble. These two icons of modern India put themselves in others' shoes. They feel for their people, whether they be employees, team members, or fellow countrymen. Both men demonstrate the same warmth, mutual respect, and sense of duty towards their team/organization and their country.

Sandeep spoke with a tone of pride, "Adversity and extreme challenges often throw up true leaders. In moments of crisis, such individuals not only show great qualities that are inherent within themselves but also nurture a culture of high commitment in the organization or team they serve in and set high standards for people to emulate. Ratan Tata is known to have once famously said, "What I would like to do is to leave behind a sustainable entity of a set of companies that operate in an exemplary manner in terms of ethics, values and continue what our ancestors left behind."

Ratan Tata's finest leadership moment came during one of India's darkest hours. The incidents that followed the 26/11 attack on Mumbai provided a sterling example of Ratan Tata's courage and commitment. "We can be hurt but cannot be knocked down," Ratan Tata said as the iconic Taj Hotel was destroyed by terrorists.

"The stories of how the staff of the Taj Hotel placed the interests of their guests above their safety demonstrated an exemplary work ethic that went beyond anything demanded by law. After the Mumbai attacks, Ratan paid the salaries of the staff, though he had to close the hotel for reconstruction. He visited families of affected employees. The Tata scion also covered compensation for railway employees, police staff, and pedestrians. He also gave grants to cover the education expenses of 46 children of victims of the terrorist attacks.

He accomplished all this with quiet dignity and without any fanfare or PR pinups.

"Leaders must evolve with time. When a style of play is successful for more than a decade, it is highly unlikely that a sportsperson will change it. In a corporate situation, for instance, many companies go out of business for precisely this reason failing to evolve according to changing market conditions." Sandeep paused to attend a phone call.

My thoughts turned to Sachin. He did adapt to changed circumstances and amended his style of batting after having spent 12 years as an ultra-attacking stroke player. He effected this change after suffering a career-threatening back injury in 1999. Until then, Tendulkar had been playing with a very heavy bat, but after the injury, a specialist advised him to use a lighter bat. That was precisely what Tendulkar did and what evolved, as a result, was a player who was probably not as much of a stroke maker as he had earlier been but a far more difficult batsman to dislodge. The ability to heed expert views and change one's approach is a quality that a true leader should possess.

Sandeep finished his call and continued from where he left, "When the Narasimha Rao government announced its economic liberalization policy in the early nineties, many Indian corporate leaders were worried because of the extended competition they would have to face. Meanwhile, Ratan Tata sensed that the policy allowed the Tata Group to expand its wings to other countries. Millions of Indians are neither employed in a Tata Group company nor do they own shares in it. Yet we all seem to have an emotional stake in the Group. Ratan is an authentic example of a leader who has painstakingly built an organization with a desire to fulfill its corporate social responsibility that goes beyond making products and services. Everyone in India seems to have an emotional stake in the Tata Group."

I added my thoughts of Sachin to the discussion, "Yes, likewise millions of us don't know Sachin Tendulkar personally. We have seen him play, and it has been a delight to watch him, but why is it that even today any news on Sachin is so emotional to all of us?" Sandeep looked amused that I still had cricket on my mind.

"Yes, true," Sandeep acknowledged, "Every Indian saw a facet of himself when he saw Sachin. It was because of the way Tendulkar presented himself, the way he treated others, and most importantly, the way he put his country and the game above himself. He remained unscathed in the most turbulent times during the match-fixing scandal. He had high values in life, and when some alcohol companies offered him a huge amount to promote their products, Sachin said, "NO."

"True humility is not thinking less of yourself; it is thinking of yourself less."

- C. S. Lewis.

"Sandeep," I said, "I am a bit confused now. We spoke about building a culture of winning mindset. How do you build a culture and manage it? Nobody likes his or her culture to be managed."

"Focus on building values that each and everyone associated with Bodhi has to buy into and they must be doable. It takes time to build an organization with a culture. So, what are our values??" Sandeep enquired. I was taken off guard.

Sandeep added, "You will never find the Tatas in the alcohol or tobacco businesses. They also never indulge in corruption or bribery. The cultural tenets of Tata can be enumerated as:

1. Unity–"We must work cohesively with our colleagues, customers, and partners around the world, building strong relationships based on tolerance and cooperation."

2. Integrity–"We must conduct our business fairly, with honesty and transparency. Everything we do must stand the test of public scrutiny."

3. Responsibility–"We must continue to be responsible and sensitive to the countries, communities, and environments in which we work, always ensuring that what comes from the people goes back to the people many times over."

4. Understanding–"We must care, show respect and compassion towards our colleagues

and customers around the world, and always work for the benefit of the communities we serve."

5. Excellence–"We must constantly strive to achieve the highest possible standards in our day-to-day work and in the quality of the goods and services we provide."

"A Tata company's management practices and business conduct shall benefit the country, localities, and communities in which it operates, to the extent possible and affordable, and shall be in accordance with the laws of the land. It shall conform to trade procedures, including licensing, documentation, and other necessary formalities."

Sandeep saw his watch and got up. "It's very late, let's continue tomorrow. I have a plan and we shall discuss in detail tomorrow over breakfast." I nodded and got up.

As I was walking to my room, my thoughts were on cricket again which I shared with Sandeep. "Sachin the cricketer and the person both conform perfectly to each of the above values adopted by the Tata Group. Tendulkar's commitment to unity and the nurturing of young talents is well known. No one has questioned his integrity, he has always accepted the responsibility of carrying the hopes of his entire team on his shoulders. Excellence is another calling sign for Sachin. With the highest number of centuries in international cricket, there cannot be a better standard-bearer of excellence."

Sandeep chipped in remarking, "Ratan Tata is the Sachin of corporate India. Indeed, he is the God of the Indian corporate world. Ratan Tata's career overlapped with that of JRD Tata. He waited for 30 long years before becoming the Chairman of the Group in 1991 when JRD stepped down. Ratan has become synonymous with the dedication and patience required to imbibe and personalize the values of the company. When Ratan took over the Tata Group in 1991, the company's market capitalization was around $1 Billion. Today, the Group employs close to 700,000 people and has a staggering revenue of over $100 billion. All this has been achieved over the last 20 years by Ratan Tata being at the helm of the Tata Group.

"Ratan Tata has redefined the business model from individualization to institutionalization, from profit to community transformation and sustainability, for setting and converging the highest standards of business probity and ethics and the highest standards of personal morality and character and for innovating constantly."
– Adi Godrej

It was that night that Bodhi's cultural values were formally seeded in that conversation. The next day at the breakfast table we decided that Bodhi would be a company that every Indian would be able to relate to with pride, emotionally own it like Tata company or Sachin. We both decided that we would broadly aim for the IPO by mid-2011 and work on building the cultural values that we have been practicing but not yet written it down.

They were:

- Meritocracy

- Integrity

- Collaboration

- Bias for Action

- Transparency

- Personal Accountability.

The above six cultural values reflected aptly what we stood for since Bodhi came into existence. These values not only found a place on every possible wall at the Bodhi offices but also in the heart of every Bodhi employee.

"We believe that it's really important to come up with the core values that you can commit to. And by commit, we mean that you're willing to hire and fire based on them. If you're willing to do that, then you're well on your way to building a company culture that is in line with the brand you want to build."

– Tony Hsieh, CEO, Zappos

Action to Readers

1. What are your core values?

2. What are your organizational values?

CHAPTER 7

Dreams Come True - 2011

India had just won the World Cup Final after 28 years and we were preparing for one of the biggest events in our lives — our IPOs. Bodhi would soon be a public limited company, one of the biggest in India.

Our operations had expanded into many areas. Our employee count stood at around 14000. We had a presence in eight other countries. Running up to our IPO, I read about all the companies in India who were noteworthy after the IPO. One company that inspired me was Reliance Industries. I was captivated by Dhirubhai Ambani's story. As India just won the World Cup, I was also following up on how Dhoni and the team won it spectacularly.

Sandeep and I met many times as we ran up to our 2011 IPO target. In one of the meetings soon after India won the World Cup, I shared with him my 'research' on Dhirubhai Ambani.

"Sandeep, I find Dhirubhai's story similar to Dhoni's in many ways. Their spirit is so contagious that today a budding cricketer or a future entrepreneur in India would feel confident that they too can succeed at the highest level if they have Determination and Dedication towards their purpose.

"Be it the corporate or cricket world, Ambani and Dhoni have proved that pedigree doesn't matter in India; performance alone matters.

Former Prime Minister Atal Behari Vajpayee described Dhirubhai Ambani as an "iconic proof of what an ordinary Indian, fired by the spirit of enterprise and driven by determination, can achieve in his lifetime." How true that statement is!

"While Dhirubhai went to Yemen and learnt about accounting and shipping, Dhoni left his native Ranchi for Kharagpur in search of a job that he eventually landed with the Indian Railways. Those journeys helped shape the careers of two prodigious men.

"Dhoni probably had the greatest number of erstwhile captains as senior players in his team — Sachin Tendulkar, Sourav Ganguly, VVS Laxman, Virender Sehwag, and Rahul Dravid — this speaks volumes for Mahi's ability to take his team along with him.

"The Indian team's run up to the 2011 World Cup win was a by-product of the focus Dhoni and the team followed. Dhoni partnered with Gary Kirsten and made some notable changes in Indian cricket. I am proud that we did something similar as we are running up to our IPO," I said.

Amused by this, Sandeep asked me, "How is it that you are comparing India's World Cup win to our IPO?"

Like a child eager to share I said, "Do you remember Sandeep in 1997 when Appa was in ICU he told us to have an aspirational goal? I think it all started there."

"At the end of 2008 when India lost to Sri Lanka, Gary Kirsten and Dhoni felt the Indian team was not playing for a purpose, it was marred with inconsistency and poor results despite having some great players. They went into a marathon huddle to find out what is it that the team wanted to achieve."

"In the huddle, Dhoni and team brainstormed what should they aspire for, and after hours of deliberation they came out with the *clarity* on their aspirational goal — India will be the World Champions in 2011."

Each member of the Indian team after that meeting, was fully brought into the larger goal of winning the World Cup in 2011. The collective goal was more important than the individual goals.

"These aspirational goals are similar to what we set out with our goal, i.e., is to create a great company and go for an IPO."

"Yeah true but it's just not *clarity* on the aspiration that got Dhoni and his men here," intervened Sandeep.

"Absolutely. However, that is the first set of things we have to do, right?" I asked.

Sandeep nodded in agreement.

"Once Dhoni had a clear purpose he went about listing the important challenges to attain that goal. His next process is interestingly similar to what we do in the corporate world.

- Who will do what and what is expected of each player was well defined - in our parlance we call it role clarity.

- Then improved each player beyond what he believed in and we call it Competency Development."

"That is an interesting observation Sanju. What competency development have you seen in Indian cricket?"

"See what Ishant Sharma did. It's not expected of No. 8, 9, 10, and 11 players to bat. They are not competent batters is the normal belief, right? These players spend more time in the nets on batting and guess what? Ishant who is considered a bowler went on to help India win a match in Mohali against Australia. Isn't that a great example of competency development?"

"Let me give you another insight," I continued, "See how Dhoni shaped Suresh Raina. Suresh is a class player but he would get out at a crucial juncture playing a loose shot. Dhoni made Gary talk to Suresh and corrected that. After that Suresh was fantastic and contributed enormously in the quarter final against Australia."

"Dhoni, while enhancing the 'People Development', simultaneously worked on incorporating the right value system and instilling the right culture. Dhoni and Gary created a happy environment and there was a strong bonding among the team members."

Sandeep responded, "Similar to Dhoni, Dhirubhai believed in relationships and trust. He famously said - between my past, present, and future, there is one common factor: Relationship and Trust. This is the foundation of our growth.

"He treated all his shareholders as an extended family and considered himself accountable to them. Reliance has grown from a small family of 58,000 shareholders to over four million. The company contributes 3% of India's GDP."

I continued. "With Gary's support, Dhoni led his team and invited Mike Horn to talk to them and inspire them. He had a simple mantra: meticulously plan & follow the process and the result will happen."

"Dhoni set goals for every department (Batting, Bowling, Fielding) along with Gary and started tracking these goals. If a match was lost, they did not focus on the result; rather they focused on which process failed and worked to correct that failure than penalize a player. This created enormous trust among the players."

Similar to Dhoni we did not have a blanket solution for all departments and people challenges. There is a significant similarity in how Dhoni handled People Development and how we did at Bodhi.

"Sanju, in summary, you are saying every leader has to define:

1. What is the team aspiring for?

2. What is the management's aspiration?

   If there is a synergy between 1 and 2, then there is goal clarity. The intensity of the synergy defines the clarity of goals.

3. Define a clear process to monitor the progress towards the goals.

4. List the challenges to attain that goal.

5. Have role clarity among teams (who will do what)

6. Enhance people's competence.

7. Create a great culture - of openness without fear to express one's views.

8. Set systems and processes that make your business profitable, scalable, and simpler.

"Yes unquestionably, and these have to be well balanced with a strategy based on situations and environment."

I could see a silent endorsement and a sense of pride in my inspiring mentor brother.

On 2nd June 2011, Bodhi made its foray into the Indian Stock Exchange. It was a big day for everyone in the company and it was indeed a dream come true for Sandeep and me.

The goal that we wrote in 1999 had come true. We have now created wealth for a lot of our employees and associates who were with Bodhi for a long time.

The BSE bell ring was an emotional ceremony with all the family present. We missed Appa a lot, the last conversation at the hospital with Appa came vividly to Sandeep and me as we did not speak a word but our eyes met, and spoke many words remembering our aspirational goal. Our issue was oversubscribed 200 times and the share price started 45% over the initial offering.

I saw a portrait of Dhirubhai Ambani and below I read the words:

Our dreams have to be bigger, our ambitions higher, our commitment deeper, and our efforts greater.

"DREAM is not what you see in sleep, DREAM is something which doesn't let you sleep."

– Dr. A.P.J Abdul Kalam

"Spend time upfront to invest in systems and processes to make long-term growth sustainable."

-Jeff Platt

Action to Readers

1. What is your World Cup/IPO Story?

2. What is your world cup kind of goal, like the one Dhoni/Gary and the Indian team created in 2008?

3. Remember winning the world cup happened on 2 April 2011 that was a result of the process that started in 2008.

4. What is your "2011 World Cup goal"?

5. Have you defined the systems and process to get there?

6. Do you have a coach like Gary to get to your goals?

7. Want to Hire your own Gary Kirsten to get your goals?

8. Want to know how to identify your coach?

Visit srikanthram.com (http://srikanthram.com)

Swami Chinmayanand said there are three kinds of people–first, those who do not start work, because of fear of obstacles. Second, those who start, but stop when they face obstacles. And third, those who work in spite of obstacles and overcome it!

Now decide which kind of person you are.

CHAPTER 8

Staying Grounded - 2014

Sandeep and I met on the sidelines of our nephew's wedding in Chennai. Looking back on our journey we were both proud of what we had achieved. Our relatives gave us special treatment. People now recognize me as some sort of celebrity and I was sharing this with Sandeep saying that I was finding it difficult to have my own space in public.

He probably suspected that the success was getting to my head and asked, "Sanju, have you heard of Azim Premji Foundation?

"The Azim Premji Foundation works to improve education in over 350,000 schools in seven states. The Azim Premji University focuses its efforts on teaching and research programs in education. Not-for-profits focused on areas such as local governance, nutrition, and the well-being of vulnerable groups can hope to get financial grants from Azim Premji Philanthropic Initiatives."

Sandeep then quoted Azim Premji, "I strongly believe that those of us, who are privileged to have wealth, should contribute significantly to try to create a better world for the millions who are far less privileged."

Sensing that I was inquisitive about Premji, Sandeep continued, "Azim Premji has shaken the corporate world by deciding to donate over a third of his company's shares to charity. While India Inc is mandated to part with 2% of their profit, Premji's generosity of transferring 67% economic ownership of the company to charity is unparalleled in the history of corporate giving and is seen with pride in India Inc."

Premji stands committed to the proverb — the more you earn the more you give.

Sandeep continued, "Apart from being a business tycoon, Premji cast himself in many roles - investor, engineer, and philanthropist, even as he led Wipro for over four decades to global leadership in information technology. With a revenue of nearly $8.5 billion, the company provides IT, BPO, and R&D services and has a presence in 58 countries."

As I heard Sandeep's narration, my mind was flashing the image of Rahul Dravid.

Dravid is synonymous with reliability. He was above all an organization man, ready to do anything to help further the interests of the team. He would don the gloves to keep wickets when the main keeper was indisposed. He was willing to turn the arm over when his skipper wanted to give the main bowlers a rest. He was a brilliant fielder and by the end of his Test career had taken 210 catches, the highest in the world. Dravid could do just about anything on the cricket field and did it all without complaining, always valuing the team's interests above everything else.

Just as Azim Premji had made an instant impact in the corporate world, so did Dravid in the cricket world, with a 95 in his debut innings followed by a fifty in the next Test. Then followed a career in which Dravid's ever-reliable presence in the Indian middle-order earned him the title of "the wall". In fact, rival teams understood that no match was won until they had got Dravid's wicket.

Once Rahul was asked about what made him happy and proud in cricket. Everybody would have thought that he would say his batting prowess and the runs he scored. But he said it was not his batting but the catches he took. Because he was able to contribute to someone's (bowler) success and the team celebrates together. Such is the spirit of this star batsman and wonderful human being.

Can anyone forget the marathon innings he played for India along with VVS Laxman in that historical Test match at Kolkata?

"Every entrepreneur can be successful. But what is important is to not let success go to your head," says Azim Premji. He has always advised young entrepreneurs to remain down to earth because the moment one lets success go to his head, he is already on his way to failure. He has also stressed the fact that failure is as much a natural phenomenon as success is. So, when you encounter failure, always learn your lesson from it and move on. Sandeep shrewdly looked at me and said, "I don't think success will go to your head."

I thought to myself, it's so true in every walk of life. In cricket too, many budding cricketers get a chance to play for the team at the national level, and then, sudden success and fame go to their heads and they gradually fade away from our minds. In the business world, an entrepreneur dreams of creating something big when he starts but eventually, he loses his way because he is battling to pay salaries to his staff, his EMIs, and misses out on building something big. It's only a few entrepreneurs who make it big and while making it big, lose their way of being grounded and giving back to society and helping the needy.

According to Premji, ordinary people can achieve extraordinary results if organized into highly charged teams. The consistent success at Wipro is largely due to Premji's pioneering focus on technology and quality of service. With his fair business dealings, Premji sought to address societal issues with an ecologically sensitive approach, leading to the recognition of Wipro's global leadership in sustainability.

Both these men have a quality of being humble which is deeply ingrained in their nature.

There cannot be a better example than Rahul Dravid for patience and perseverance. At the end of his career, he had accumulated over 13000 runs in Tests. Though he played 36 matches lesser than Sachin Tendulkar, Dravid set a world record by facing more deliveries and spending more time at the crease than any other batsman in Test cricket. This statistic alone demonstrates how well he had protected the Indian innings from collapse time and again. Moreover, he was the only Indian batsman with a better average in overseas conditions, underscoring his ability to play on any surface and against any bowling attack.

Today Dravid actively guides youngsters. In 2014, Bangalore's GoSports Foundation welcomed Dravid as a member of their advisory board. India's future Olympians and Paralympians are being mentored as part of the Rahul Dravid Athlete Mentorship Programme with collaborative help from the GoSports Foundation. Young sportspersons who have benefited from Dravid's mentoring efforts include shuttler Prannoy Kumar, para-swimmer Sharath Gayakwad, and golfer S. Chikkarangappa. The BCCI has recognized Dravid's willingness to give back to the sport as much as, or even more than, he had gained from it. Rahul Dravid was appointed as head of the National Cricket Academy in 2009, to oversee the development of the India A, Under-19, and Under-23 teams. The role also requires Dravid to work closely with the head coaches of national men's and women's teams.

If the future is bright, whether of India Inc or Indian cricket, much credit must go to the contributions of these two legends, Azim Premji and Rahul Dravid respectively.

Premji's benevolence of donating thrice the mandated Corporate Social Responsibility (CSR) of Indian corporates is likely to inspire many corporates to pursue magnanimity and likely to up the ante for a new corporate order with a renewed CSR.

Sandeep summarized, "Philanthropic initiatives lead to greater customer engagement by making the connection between the company, the customer experience, and community building. Like employees, customers too want to feel good about the companies they interact with."

After this inspiring insight, we decided to pledge 40% of our net worth to help budding entrepreneurs and another 20% towards philanthropy.

Humanity will remember some men forever, simply because they made the world a better place to live in than it was when they first set foot on it.

"Keep your eyes on the stars, and your feet on the ground."

—Theodore Roosevelt

Action to readers

1. What is your contribution to society?

2. Have you ever realized that the human soul attains more happiness by giving than receiving?

3. How consistent is your contribution?

I must thank you for reading this far and importantly for patronizing this book. 10% of the proceeds of this book will go towards charity.

Heartfelt thank you for your contribution.

CHAPTER 9

Women Power – 2015

Tara, my daughter, like me has taken up cricket and is crazy about it. She enjoys the game a lot and was coming up as a fine all-rounder. She is just 12 years and is working hard to find a place in the under-14 Stateside.

I was proud of her achievements and felt happy that women's cricket is catching up in the country. Sandeep was very appreciative of Tara's achievements not only in cricket but also in academics. Sandeep asked Tara as to who her idol was. Without giving it any further thought she said, "Mithali Raj in Cricket and Appa in Business." I could feel Sandeep was emotional, thinking of me in the olden days.

"So, do you want to foray into a business too like Appa?" asked Sandeep.

"Yes, after I complete playing for India, my ambition is to get into the business," said little Tara confidently.

Sandeep was interacting a lot with Vani Kola of Kalaari Capital after we decided to help startups significantly. Vani is a pioneer in this field and was already helping a lot of young entrepreneurs achieve their dreams.

Sandeep was fondly advising and encouraging Tara. "Women need to have a long list of skill sets. For instance, I see a lot of women who want to run a business, develop a liking for maths, be willing to embrace technology, and most importantly, be ready to rough it out in business. And not to mention the need to manage a family."

Sandeep was sharing information on Vani, "Vani has done all of this, and more, to set an example for all young women who aspire to run businesses. She is a pioneer in Venture capital and has run up a list of enviable investments in such startup unicorns as Flipkart, Myntra, Zivame, Urban Ladder, Bluestone, and Snap Deal. Hailing from a Brahmin family, Vani began her career in the US. She started business enterprises there before deciding to return to India with her family to invest in Indian startups. She leveraged her ability to identify smart entrepreneurs, mentor them, and back them in the running of their businesses - not an easy thing to do. Vani has proven herself to be a luminary icon in the startup environment."

Sandeep asked Tara why she chose Mithali as her idol.

Tara enthusiastically replied, "Mithali Raj is the first women's cricket captain to lead India to the ICC ODI World Cup final. In fact, she did it twice, the first time in 2005 and then again in 2017. She is the highest run-scorer in women's ODIs, having amassed 6190 runs. The Government of India recognized Mithali's achievements and conferred her with an Arjuna Award in 2003. Thanks to Mithali's exploits, she has received what is arguably the greatest compliment any woman cricketer could hope to receive: she is called the Sachin Tendulkar of Indian Women's Cricket.

"Very true Tara, both these inspiring women possess one striking skill set: the power of self belief," Sandeep asserted, "Never lose self-belief in any situation."

Vani described it succinctly. "Self-doubt can poison success, but belief can open the universe. Every journey starts with a dream, idea, or vision. What we as the audience get to see is that vision or dream when achieved but we never get an insight (into) the fight, the trauma, the pain, the stress, the strain a person has to go through, and if it's a woman, it's even more respectable."

As these interesting conversations between Sandeep and Tara were taking place, I remembered reading an article on Mithali Raj, especially on her Determination.

Mithali's India story may have been cut short in its glory. A knee injury in 2009 threatened to cut short her cricket career but the women's cricket legend was never going to give up without a fight. She spent hundreds of hours in physiotherapy to ensure that she was up and running.

In early 2000, at a time when BCCI had not yet brought Indian Women's Cricket under its authority, and when the women's game was bereft of sponsors, Mithali used to travel in unreserved compartments and stay in dorms. More often,

Mithali wanted to quit the game because she was all alone on a man's turf and often had to practice with men as there were no women's teams. Given that Indian Women's Cricket did not have a budget, there would be just one series the entire year round, when a visiting team came to India. To stay in that circuit and shine for 20 years is no mean achievement.

In today's world where IQ (intelligent quotient), EQ (emotional quotient), and even Spiritual Quotient is important the relevance of Adaptability Quotient (AQ) is also increasing rapidly.

The ability to adapt to various situations is another mantra that these leaders have demonstrated, and this ability has been achieved through a combination of hard work, discipline, self-confidence, and the will to dream big. There is no doubt that her technical skills and mental toughness went a long way in making Mithali the most promising woman player in India.

She took her game to the next level to become one of the world's finest women cricketers with the ability to adapt to situations. In the process, she broke Karen Rolton's record for the highest individual score in Test cricket, when she smashed the barrier of 209 to set her high mark of 214 against England. Mithali also established the still unbroken record of seven consecutive half-centuries. She has combined the ability to score quick runs with the penchant for staying calm and composed in critical situations.

Sandeep pointed out, "Kalaari Capital began operations as a US$150 million fund in September 2012. Under Vani's leadership, the firm registered a four-fold growth; as of 2017, the fund had assets valued at US$650 million."

According to Vani, an entrepreneur is a person who not only creates jobs for the masses but also generates wealth and shares that wealth with many. Such should be the goal of entrepreneurs. It's a matter of time before many companies in India will produce entrepreneurs with such a mindset. Women make better entrepreneurs, and in the last decade in India, we have witnessed more and more women taking the hot seat and creating jobs and wealth. Vani will be the torch-bearer, inspiring many women entrepreneurs in the foreseeable future to come forward to show us all how to lead and create wealth."

Indian Men's Cricket is flourishing and Women's Cricket is not far behind.

There is a very talented crop of players in Harmanpreet Kaur, Smriti Mandana, Veda Krishnamurthy, and Jemimah Rodrigues who are taking the Indian flag in Women's Cricket higher, and soon we will be seeing Women's IPL.

Now 38, Mithali is still active in ODIs and dreams of winning the World Cup for India.

Indian Women's Cricket has just begun to produce many prospective legends in the years to come, and when we will look back, we will recognize Mithali's story as the one that started it all.

"Women are the largest untapped reservoir of talent in the world."

-Hillary Clinton

Action to readers

1. When are the times in your life you had Self Doubts?

2. List down the times you have adapted to the situations and succeeded?

CHAPTER 10

Finding Harmony – 2018

In June 2011, soon after India won the World Cup, I had an opportunity to meet Gary Kirsten, the erstwhile coach of the winning Indian team. I asked him why he had resigned as a coach soon after India won the World Cup. Kirsten could easily have continued for a few more years while attracting lucrative contracts. But he said something that will forever stay with me. He said leaders must know when to go and hand over the reins to the younger generation.

It was something that I wanted to discuss with Sandeep at the earliest. It was important to me that we find the right person to pass on the baton. I have been reading a lot in the media. No matter how good a leader an individual might grow up to be, he will be less effective if there is a giant gap between the expectations of the promoters/top management and his performance. There are several instances — in both the corporate arena and cricket — of highly qualified and successful leaders who were sacked when their actions were perceived by the promoters as going against the interests of the organization.

Gary Kirsten's words have been ringing in my ears time and again, and made me think about who is after me, not that I have become old but the baton change and grooming another leader was always on my mind. I also someday wanted to hand over the reins of running the day-to-day affairs of the company and help young entrepreneurs who were struggling in their earlier careers but had immense potential to make it big.

I started discussing this with Sandeep when we met in Delhi. It was a big day for Sandeep as he was being awarded by the CII for his contribution to the industry.

"Sandeep, I have been giving a lot of thought about who would take over from me to run the day-to-day business. We have to appoint someone who blends well with the organization's aspirations and culture or else it will be a colossal disaster."

My mind as usual went to see the parallels in cricket. I told Sandeep, "Saurav Ganguly who took over from Tendulkar in 2000 enjoyed a successful tenure as captain of India. His accomplishments included winning the Champions Trophy in 2002, leading India to the World Cup final in 2003, and many Test wins abroad. All of these achievements came during John Wright's tenure as coach of the national squad.

"However, a relatively mediocre 2004-05 season saw Wright choosing not to renew his contract as a coach. Greg Chappell took over as India's coach, the first series on his watch was in Zimbabwe. Matters became worse after a leaked email from Chappell to the BCCI in which he is alleged to have questioned Ganguly's suitability for the captaincy.

"At this point, Ganguly was undergoing a poor run with the bat, and that did not help his cause. As things transpired, Dada not only lost his captaincy but was also dropped from the team, though he did return as a team member in January 2006. But his inconsistent form with the bat continued, leading to the eventual end of his career in 2008."

"You do understand, what I am trying to tell you? We need to appoint someone who knows how to establish a harmonious relationship with the stakeholders, and also knows when to let go of their position for the next generation," I told Sandeep.

Sandeep and I had established very early in our careers that we would be helping young entrepreneurs take the centre stage after us. It was an important commitment for us - we were young, naïve entrepreneurs who were very apprehensive about entering the corporate arena. We lacked a proper mentor, and we wanted to fill that void in a newbie entrepreneur's life.

"I understand, Sanju and I highly respect the fact that you are giving this so much importance. You must have heard of Vishal Sikka and Cyrus Mistry?"

"When Narayana Murthy decided to step down as CEO at Infosys, Sikka's technological acumen contributed largely to his appointment as NRN's successor. Vishal Sikka's stay at the top in Infosys did not last very long either. Taking over from the interim CEO, SD Shibulal, in June 2014, Sikka had to vacate the post three years later in August 2017. Many decisions taken by the company's board under Sikka's leadership appear not to have gone down well with the founders of the company who continue to own about 16% of the shares."

"The fact that Infosys under Sikka shifted away from traditional IT services is considered being chief among these areas of disagreement. Disputes over a pay rise to Sikka as well as over the size of severance packages to the company's employees only contributed to the disenchantment."

"Take the instance of Cyrus Mistry. In 1991, Mistry joined his family business (Shapoorji Pallonji) as a Director. In 2013, he was dubbed "the most important industrialist in India and Britain" by The Economist. Mistry's experience on the board of several Tata Companies made him a prime candidate to take over from Ratan Tata when Ratan decided to step down as Chairman and MD in 2013."

"Mistry stayed at the helm for four years at Tata Sons, when the Board decided that he would have to go. Several decisions made by Mistry appear to have gone against the wishes of other Board members. Subsequently, six of nine Board members voted to have Mistry removed from the helm, while two abstained. (Mistry himself was not allowed to vote on the motion.) Speculation in the media attributed Mistry's ouster to falling profits in several Tata Group companies, the subsequent sale of many group assets, and a failed joint venture effort with Docomo, a Japanese telecom company."

"You can have the highest degrees but still fail to keep up with an organization's aspirations and values. Primarily there is disharmony and misalignment of objectives between the promoters."

"We have to choose an able successor," Sandeep said, but it has to be meticulously planned and executed."

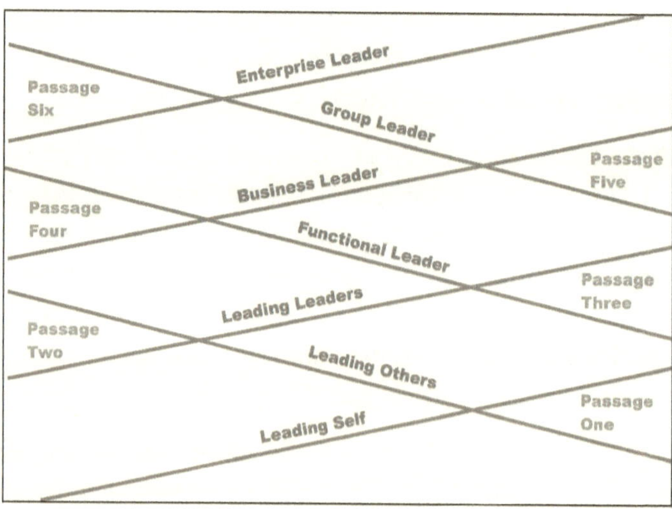

"So, what is the plan and how do we go about it?" I asked.

"One of the well-tested models for leadership pipeline building is advocated by Ram Charan, the famous Management guru and I think we should adopt that," said Sandeep and elaborated.

"Charan describes seven levels of leadership with **SIX TRANSITIONS OF LEADERSHIP** in between. The best leaders in every organization are the leaders who have grown through each of these levels, to learn the values and skills on their way to the next level."

I realised that we had the big task on our hands to select an able successor, to ensure our brainchild Bodhi's long harmonious future.

"The way a team plays as a whole determines its success. You may have the greatest bunch of individual stars in the world, but if they don't play together, the club won't be worth a dime."

– Babe Ruth

Action to readers

1. Are you ready with your second line?

2. Are you grooming your next set of leaders to take your position?

3. Are you constantly looking to become obsolete in your current position?

CHAPTER 11

Baton Change - 2019

Sandeep and I have always been keen on supporting the dreams of budding entrepreneurs. We started with zero guidance and we knew how tough it was to make it big in the corporate world. We wanted to hand over the reins of operating the day-to-day functioning of the company to someone so that we could devote ourselves to the former cause.

We applied the principles of Ram Charan and for over a year we were contemplating a successor. After careful deliberations, we selected Bharat Malli to take over as the CEO and I would continue as Chairman Emeritus.

Bharat Malli was our Head of Operations. Over the years Malli had become Bodhi's most trusted member. His adherence to our company culture and great strategy planning had made him one of the most outstanding members of Bodhi. Sandeep and I decided that it would be best for our company to be run by him; while we fulfilled our duty of helping the budding entrepreneurs.

With the decision to put Bharat at the wheel, we decided to plunge right in. Sandeep and I heard about numerous successful entrepreneurs who had helped and motivated budding entrepreneurs to build successful business empires. A lot has been talked about the benefits of the proverbial silver spoon, whether in business, arts, or sports. A lot less has been talked about the pressure of expectation that weighs on these spoon holders. They are not only expected to reach the levels achieved by their predecessors but are expected to go beyond them. The pressure of the achievements of their predecessors is so huge that failure ceases to be an option; consequently, failure becomes a real possibility.

"Before you begin coaching entrepreneurs outside, you must ensure Bharat is well supported and handheld by you at least for six months," said Sandeep. We decided to call Bharat and tell him about our decision that he would take over as the new CEO and if he had any thoughts on the same.

Bharat was delighted that we had selected him to be the new CEO, but he was modest. "Sir, it will be difficult to fill in your shoes, but I assure you I will do my best," he said.

Sandeep intervened, "Bharat, you have all the qualities to lead Bodhi to the next level. But I don't want you to just fill in the shoes of Sanju, you need to surpass."

"Yes, I am aware, for somebody to come out of the shadow of a stalwart is a Herculean task — and push the envelope further to become a legend himself, such an individual would need to conform to a different level of hard work, dedication, and zeal to perform at the highest level. If one succeeds, though, the new benchmarks created by such a leader will make it even more exciting and challenging for future leaders to emulate them."

I always felt pride and a deep sense of gratitude when Sandeep acknowledged my work.

"The levels that such an individual will set will define a new normal, and the community whether relating to business or sports will scale a new level of excellence for others to attain and go beyond. It's not an easy challenge, but that is precisely why it is important."

Sandeep continued, "Mukesh Ambani and Virat Kohli are classic examples of such a rare breed who have not only reached the level of excellence achieved by their illustrious predecessors but have gone beyond it to create their legacy."

Mukesh took over the reins of Reliance Industries (RIL) when the legendary Dhirubhai Ambani passed away in July 2002. By that time, Mukesh had been in the company since 1981 and spent over 20 years working alongside his father. When Dhirubhai passed away, Reliance had a turnover of INR 75,000 crore and by then it was the first Indian company to be featured in the Global Fortune 500 list. Mukesh Ambani's taking over the reins of the business from this substantial position and transforming it to make Reliance what it is today has been a truly remarkable achievement.

"With new business strategies and the acumen to adapt rapidly to a changing environment in a VUCA world — a world full of volatility, uncertainty, complexity, ambiguity — RIL is setting itself up for the next big haul. The success of Mukesh Ambani has been nothing less than extraordinary. Whether it relates to polyester or fuel or retail or the new business of Jio, the consumer reach in each of these categories has been phenomenal. In his pursuit of success, Mukesh has not deviated from the core values of Reliance that were established by his illustrious father. And that is a basic quality that we expect of a true leader who upholds the values that Bodhi stands for."

An avowed core value of the Reliance Group is that businesses should have larger purposes. Businesses are not judged merely by their balance sheets but also by the way they work to ensure the betterment of society. Reliance Foundation, headed by Mukesh Ambani's wife Nita Ambani, renders yeoman service in the areas of Rural Transformation, Health, Education, Sports for Development, Disaster Response, Arts, Culture & Heritage, and Urban Renewal. The foundation also uses the money raised towards the education and healthcare of underprivileged children.

Sandeep had always marveled at Mukesh Ambani's talent and perseverance and I admired Virat Kohli for his grit and aggression and most importantly leading from the front.

The story of Virat Kohli was even more dramatic. Captainship came naturally to Virat Kohli. However, to take over the reins from a legendary leader like Dhoni must have been overwhelming. In early 2015, when Virat Kohli became the permanent captain of the Tests, India was ranked 7th in Tests, above only the West Indies, Bangladesh, and Zimbabwe. That was an absolute low for India. He arrived on the scene as an under-19 World Cup winning captain who was talented and flamboyant.

He was also way heavier then and also lacked work ethics. The glamour of IPL looked likely to ruin him; it appeared a world-class talent was about to get wasted. However, luckily for the world of cricket, sometime around 2012, Virat looked at himself in a mirror and decided that his physical condition was not up to international standards. If Virat had to make a mark in international cricket, he would have to effect a dramatic transformation. He did transform, Kohli not only lost weight but gained core strength as well. He worked countless hours in the nets. Virat wasn't as talented as a Sachin Tendulkar or a Ricky Ponting but made up for the lack with an extraordinary work ethic and amazing determination. He made chasing his forte, becoming one of the greatest chasers and arguably one of the greatest batsmen in ODI cricket.

Despite having a good squad and a great cricketing legacy, India was lingering at the bottom of the rankings. Virat took over the captaincy with a very positive mindset. He realized the importance of away wins. He also acknowledged that to win away from home he needed to focus more on grooming fast bowlers. He cultivated a culture of fitness and led by example, maintaining himself as one of the fittest in the team. He always placed greater emphasis on the process than on the outcome.

By the time he was done assembling the team he wanted, India was virtually impregnable at home and eventually winning away from home. Virat emerged from the shadows of the great Dhoni and created a niche for himself. He became one of the finest cricketers India has ever produced by dint of sheer determination, game sense, and willingness to adapt to change. Virat has always put the victory of the team ahead of personal milestones and has been vocal about it in the media as well. He has cultivated and enhanced a culture wherein a larger purpose is more significant than an individual record.

Like Mukesh Ambani, Virat has great respect for his predecessors and has always been humble in acknowledging their contributions. He doesn't hesitate to consult his seniors in the team when needed and honestly attributes the success of his decisions to them - a characteristic of a true leader. While the team has been improving, Virat himself has improved tenfold. The way he is going, he will have many batting records, by the time he retires.

Sandeep told Bharat with emphasis, "Mukesh Ambani and Virat Kohli inherited a great legacy, while they also had the pressure of creating their own. Both have done pretty well and continue to do so. I want you to emulate this in Bodhi and carve out your own space in the leadership.

"The final test of greatness in a CEO is how well he chooses a successor and whether he can step aside and let the successor run the company."

-Peter Drucker

Action to readers

1. Do you have clarity of plans for how your business will be shaped and handed over to the next generation?

2. Have you prepared yourself to pass the baton?

CHAPTER 12

Winning at What Cost- 2020

"**A**ppa I want to come with you to attend the Town Hall," said my daughter Tara. It was our quarterly Town Hall that I address, updating everyone on the progress of Bodhi and what we would do in the following quarter. At this meet, I chose to announce to all the employees about the appointment of Bharat as the new CEO.

It would be my last quarterly Town Hall. The previous day, we had announced at our leadership team meeting consisting of all HODs about Bharat and it was unanimously supported by all. It showed the respect Bharat had earned among his peers.

I announced to the entire team of over 20,000 from across 120 countries about Bharat's appointment. It was welcomed with a loud cheer. I wanted to make it a memorable one, not only for me but for each one of them.

It's the people who make the difference in any organisation. I wanted every member of Bodhi to understand our values and what we stand for.

I spoke extempore, "What is our organizational culture? Is it the values we have put up on the wall? How do we win in the marketplace? Is it to win at all costs? What decides an excellent place to work in? Is it the brand value of an organization and compensation paid to employees?

"I firmly believe that you can take a product and people out of an organization, but you can never take the culture out.

"Many experts believe that it's the culture of an organization; the organizational philosophy and belief system that is the heart and soul of an organization; this is what helps to retain people and binds them to it.

"Sandeep and I had been extremely cautious about building an extremely great work culture in Bodhi. Culture plays a vital role in shaping an organization and its ability to withstand the pressures of its external environment.

"Peter Drucker, the renowned management guru said — Culture eats strategy for breakfast. No matter how effective your strategy sounds, the culture of your organisation is the supreme determinant factor behind its success."

"Take the example of Satyam Computers which was an iconic company boasting of 185 Fortune 500 companies among its clients. On 7 January 2009, the Chairman of Satyam, Ramalinga Raju, resigned, admitting to having fudged the accounts for Rs 14,162 crore in various ways. The episode shocked the global corporate community.

"What caused Ramalinga Raju to fudge the books? If you analyse carefully, you will see that Raju, and, by implication, Satyam had compromised the ethics of doing business. No code of conduct existed in the organization as the members of top management themselves–including the chairman– were wilfully involved in fraudulent transactions. Satyam's shares fell from Rs 544 in 2008 to Rs 11.50 on 10 January 2009.

"As someone with great interest in cricket, I can assure that culture plays an important role not only in the corporate world but also in cricket.

"Take for instance, what happened with Steve Smith and the Australian team during their tour of South Africa in March 2018. During the third Test match of the four-match series at Newlands in Cape Town, TV cameras caught Cameron Bancroft using sandpaper to rough up one side of the ball to make the ball swing.

"Cricket Australia later found Captain Steve Smith and vice-captain David Warner complicit and punished the players with unprecedented sanctions.

"Australian cricket had gained a good reputation for professionalism and precision in the execution of strategy. No thanks to the shenanigans of Smith and company, Australian cricket was reduced to humiliation and shame.

I don't believe the Smith incident is a one-off case or an aberration.

"It's more likely the culmination of the organizational culture created by the Australian Cricket Board. Australian cricketers have always carried a bit of arrogance in their playing style what we know as Sledging. Who can forget the monkey gate episode or the image of Smith turning to the dressing room if he had to go for a review?

"Australian Cricket administration has failed to make it clear to its players what is acceptable behaviour and what is not. The Steve Smith flashpoint came after the situation had got exacerbated over a period during which the players were given to understand that it was okay to win any which way. Winning was all that mattered. How the victory was achieved did not matter in the least," I said.

"If only they were taught better values, that would have saved them from the disrespect they faced.

"We learn another important lesson from this. In his press conference after the episode, Steve Smith, the disgraced captain of Australia's cricket team, made it sound like an ordinary meeting of a sales team discussing how to capture a higher market share."

"We spoke about it and thought it was a viable way of getting an advantage." He had formed a 'leadership team' consisting only of himself and his deputy. They got busy creating a strategy to beat South Africa rather than playing by the rules.

"They opted for ball-tampering – altering the surface of the ball so that it moves in the air in unexpected ways. Like a coward, Smith said, 'Obviously, it didn't work.' If you always stick around with just a few colleagues, all of whom think the same way, then some unchallenged ideas you may hatch are bound to be wrong. In the heat of a competitive battle, a few may even be ethically wrong. As an organisation, we have to pay attention to alternate views and encourage diversity," I said.

Sandeep had a proud smile on his face and shook his head in approval. "As leaders of an organization, we must make it clear about what is valued and what will not be tolerated, and we must communicate that regularly. It is just not enough to have a mission statement on a poster or to write a 'zero-tolerance policy' and stick it on a Wikipedia write-up.

"The ideology of an organization is what constitutes its work culture. Such culture affects or defines the ability of the leadership and employees to relate to each other for the common good of the organization and to operate within a mutually agreed and acceptable boundary of cultural values and emotional interface.

"It is widely understood that a positive ambience can make or mar your performance, be it in school, college, or the workplace. No matter how talented and smart you are, you cannot work to the best of your capabilities and creative skills if you are not surrounded by an encouraging environment that values human resources.

"That is why work culture is so vital in bringing out the best from your employees, even in the most adverse circumstances. Negativity not only kills creativity and the will to perform but also does not allow an employee to develop a sense of ownership and affection towards the organization.

"Competence at the workplace is a great virtue, but such competence carries little value if it's not accompanied by integrity and uncompromising loyalty to the organization.

"We have to create a positive environment and imbibe the best values in our employees.

"As I sign off, there is one question that many people have asked me over the years, why we named the company "Bodhi". This would summarise the journey so far and the years to come.

"You all know that Bodhi is the state of enlightenment attained by a Buddhist who has practiced the Eightfold Path and attained salvation. What is this eight-fold path and what is that got to do with our company."

In brief, the eight elements of the path are:

1. **Correct view**, an accurate understanding of the nature of things, specifically the Four Noble Truths.

    We will always have the correct view of our customer's needs and serve them.

2. **Correct intention**, avoiding thoughts of attachment, hatred, and harmful intent

    We will have the right intention that is to create value for all stakeholders-customers, employees, and shareholders.

3. **Correct speech**, refraining from verbal misdeeds such as lying, divisive speech, harsh speech, and senseless speech,

    We will have transparency in what we do and communicate the truth at all times.

4. **Correct action**, refraining from physical misdeeds such as killing, stealing, and sexual misconduct,

    We will not involve in any business or process that is illegal or against law.

5. **Correct livelihood**, avoiding trades that directly or indirectly harm others, such as selling slaves, weapons, animals for slaughter, intoxicants, or poisons,

    Our Employees are our Assets and we will strive to give the best livelihood to all our employees.

6. **Correct effort**, abandoning negative states of mind that have already arisen, preventing negative states that have yet to arise, and sustaining positive states that have already arisen,

We will compete fairly and play fairly at all times.

7.   **Correct mindfulness**, awareness of body, feelings, thought, and phenomena (the constituents of the existing world), and

We will be aware of nature and strive to achieve sustainability in all we do.

8.   **Correct concentration**, single-mindedness.

We will single-mindedly have our customer at the center of our decision making.

Tara sat quietly and listened to the entire speech. I was proud to see her take an active interest in the company's culture and further growth. I could see the next leader in her eyes, and that filled me with a sense of pride.

A positive company culture that helps you thrive and grow is very important. No matter how talented and competent your employees are, if your company stands on illicit activities, anti-diversity rules and regulations, and an extremely negative base; it will never succeed in making it large in the corporate world and will forever be called a poor example. Be bold to highlight any wrongdoing at any level by anybody. I leave this delicate aspect of culture in each of your hands.

Thank you.

I could hear the thunderous applause and standing ovation, something that I could not get in the cricket arena. I waved like Sachin Tendulkar's classic image of holding his bat up and seeing up the sky in gratitude. Gratitude to his father every time he hit a century. I did the same, just that I did not have a bat in my hand. But I knew my Appa's blessing was with me as I remembered the night in ICU.

"That is your legacy on this Earth when you leave this Earth: how many hearts you touched."

—*Patti Davis*

Dear Reader,

Hope you enjoyed the reading. I have a request. Cricket has travelled/travelling with us. We may have played or just been an avid follower of this great game. We are passionate about this beautiful game. Many of us have some memories or other.

I want you to pen down your memories about this game and the story that attaches to you in your life.

What emotions have been associated with this game for you?

Please write to us with your stories, we will compile all stories and publish.

The stories will be in your name and I will just compile and publish various interesting stories.

Please write to connect@srikanthram.com (mailto:connect@ srikanthram.com) or visit the website srikanthram.com (http://srikanthram.com) and upload your stories there.

Thank you.

Srikanth Ram

About the Author

Srikanth Ram has over two decades of work experience with various top corporates in India. He has worked for over a decade with Raymond as a Business head. He is an in-demand goal coach. He loves helping entrepreneurs and leaders to build high-performance teams and a winning culture. He also helps individuals to find their life goals and live a life of purpose.

Srikanth has worked in the corporate world for various Indian and multinational companies in product development, planning, sales, sourcing, design, and quality assurance. He has facilitated leadership development and encouraged multiple teams to scale to high performance for the last two decades in both his entrepreneurial and corporate careers.

His passion for cricket and a unique outlook on the game has helped him achieve his goals and get a better understanding of what it takes to lead.

He is a certified advanced paragliding pilot, marathoner, fitness enthusiast, and an avid yoga practitioner.

Srikanth lives in Mumbai, India, with his wife Poornima, cricketer daughter Ria, and a poodle Mojo.

Index

A

AB Group 60
Adaptability Quotient 101
Aditya Birla 59
Atal Behari Vajpayee 83
Australia 15, 61, 72, 85, 120, 121
Azim Premji 91, 92, 93, 96

B

Bluestone 99
Brett Lee 72

C

Cameron Bancroft 120
connected leader 65, 70, 72
culture 1, 3, 11, 12, 13, 74, 77, 80, 86, 87, 105, 111, 115, 116, 119, 120, 121, 122, 123, 125, 128
Cyrus Mistry 106, 107

D

Dada 59, 60, 61, 62, 106
David Warner 120
decision making 125
Dedication 83

Determination 83, 100
Dhirubhai Ambani 82, 83, 88, 113
Dhoni 15, 61, 62, 71, 72, 82, 83, 84, 85, 86, 89, 114, 116
Docomo 108
Dravid 61, 62, 92, 93, 95

E

Eightfold Path 37, 123
England 72, 101
entrepreneur 7, 83, 93, 94, 102, 106
EQ 101

F

Flipkart 99

G

Ganguly 59, 61, 62, 105, 106
Gary 83, 84, 85, 86, 89, 104, 105
Gary Kirsten 83, 84, 89, 104, 105
goals 70, 84, 86, 87, 89, 128
Golem effect 64
GoSports Foundation 95
Greg Chappell 105

H

Harbhajan 61
Harmanpreet Kaur 102
humility 73, 76

I

Iceberg Model 56

Ikigai 39, 40, 43

India 9, 14, 15, 60, 61, 62, 71, 72, 73, 74, 76, 78, 82, 83, 84, 85, 86, 92, 93, 95, 96, 98, 99, 100, 101, 102, 104, 105, 107, 115, 116, 128

Infosys 106, 107

Integrity 77, 80

IPL 102, 115

IPO 36, 73, 79, 82, 84, 89

IQ 101

Ishant Sharma 85

J

Jemimah Rodrigues 102

Joginder 71

Justin Langer 49

K

Kalaari 98, 102

Karen Rolton 101

KMB 59, 60, 61, 62

L

leadership 10, 11, 13, 14, 59, 61, 62, 65, 74, 92, 94, 102, 107, 109, 116, 118, 121, 122, 128

M

Michael Hussey 72

Mithali 98, 99, 100, 101, 102

Mithali Raj 98, 99, 100
MNC 30
Mukesh Ambani 113, 114, 116
Myntra 99

N

Narasimha Rao 75
Narayana Murthy 106
National Cricket Academy 95
NRN 106

P

Pakistan 14, 62, 71, 72
Paulo Coelho 42
performance 1, 3, 11, 13, 64, 83, 104, 122, 128
Prannoy Kumar 95
Premji 91, 92, 94, 96
purpose 15, 60, 63, 68, 69, 70, 83, 84, 85, 116
Pygmalion effect 64

R

Rahul Dravid 62, 83, 92, 95, 96
Ramalinga Raju 119, 120
Ram Charan 109, 111
Ratan Tata 73, 74, 75, 78, 79, 107
Reliance Foundation 114
Reliance Industries 82, 113
RIL 114
RP Singh 15, 72

S

Sachin 59, 61, 73, 75, 76, 78, 79, 83, 95, 100, 115, 125
Sachin Tendulkar 59, 73, 76, 83, 95, 100, 115, 125
Satyam Computers 119
S. Chikkarangappa 95
Shapoorji Pallonji 107
Sharath Gayakwad 95
Sharma 14, 71
Sikka 106, 107
SIX TRANSITIONS OF LEADERSHIP 109
Smith 120, 121, 122
Smriti Mandana 102
Snap Deal 99
Sourav Ganguly 83
South Africa 62, 71, 120, 121
Spiritual Quotient 101
Sri Lanka 84
Steve 120, 121
Suresh 15, 58, 85
Swami Vivekananda 68

T

Taj Hotel 74
Tata Group 14, 75, 78, 79, 107
Tony Hsieh 80

U

Urban Ladder 99

V

Vani 98, 99, 100, 102
Vani Kola 98
Veda Krishnamurthy 102
Virat Kohli 15, 113, 114, 116
Virender Sehwag 61, 62, 83
Vishal Sikka 106
VVS Laxman 24, 83, 93

W

Wipro 92, 94
World Cup 15, 71, 82, 83, 84, 89, 99, 102, 104, 105, 115

Z

Zaheer 61
Zappos 80
Zimbabwe 106, 115
Zivame 99